SETTING UP IN INDEPEN

Professional Handbooks in Counselling and Psychotherapy

This series of professional handbooks is designed for trainees as well as practitioners in the field of psychological therapy, counselling, emotional wellbeing and mental health. It focuses on key areas of practice interest and training need.

The books are characterised by:

■ their pluralistic and undogmatic approach to theory – theoretically informed, they maintain a flexible view about what works for whom;
■ their practical stance – the books all focus on the guidance professionals need in order to optimise their skill and effectiveness;
■ their easy-to-use format – they are clearly structured in order to aid navigation and employ devices such as vignettes, transcripts, checklists and reflective questions to support the reader in deepening their understanding of the main issues.

Published

Robert Bor, Sheila Gill, Riva Miller and Amanda Evans
Counselling in Health Care Settings: A Handbook for Practitioners

Robert Bor and Anne Stokes
Setting up in Independent Practice: A Handbook for Therapy and Psychology Practitioners

Susy Churchill
The Troubled Mind: A Handbook of Therapeutic Approaches to Psychological Distress

Gill Jones and Anne Stokes
Online Counselling: A Handbook for Practitioners

Setting up in Independent Practice

A Handbook for Counsellors, Therapists and Psychologists

Robert Bor
Anne Stokes

First published 2011 by
PALGRAVE MACMILLAN

Palgrave Macmillan in the UK is an imprint of Macmillan Publishers Limited,
registered in England, company number 785998, of Houndmills, Basingstoke,
Hampshire RG21 6XS.

Palgrave Macmillan in the US is a division of St Martin's Press LLC,
175 Fifth Avenue, New York, NY 10010.

Palgrave Macmillan is the global academic imprint of the above companies
and has companies and representatives throughout the world.

Palgrave® and Macmillan® are registered trademarks in the United States,
the United Kingdom, Europe and other countries

ISBN 978–0–230–24195–4

This book is printed on paper suitable for recycling and made from fully
managed and sustained forest sources. Logging, pulping and manufacturing
processes are expected to conform to the environmental regulations of the
country of origin.

A catalogue record for this book is available from the British Library.

A catalog record for this book is available from the Library of Congress.

10 9 8 7 6 5 4 3 2 1
20 19 18 17 16 15 14 13 12 11

Printed and bound in Great Britain by
CPI Antony Rowe, Chippenham and Eastbourne

Contents

Acknowledgements

We dedicate this book to all of our professional colleagues and to the clients with whom we have each had the privilege to work during our careers.

We are fortunate in having supportive and inspiring colleagues in the many different contexts in which we have worked: The Royal Free Hospital, Hampstead Group Practice, London Oncology Clinic, The London Clinic, University of Bristol, and North Hampshire Counselling Network.

A book of this kind is always the product of wider collaboration and learning and we are especially grateful to the following colleagues for sharing their time and experience with us over many years: Tim Bond, Hazel Johns, Jane Speedy, Sheila Trahar, Sheila Gill, Peter du Plessis, Peter Scragg, Carina Eriksen, Brett Kahr, Janet Reibstein, Linda Papadopoulos, Riva Miller and Ricky Snyders.

Our own supervisees have started their own journeys into independent practice and their confidence in us as colleagues and mentors is appreciated and also helped to sharpen our own thoughts and reflections as we've written this book. Finally, our editor at Palgrave Macmillan, Catherine Gray, has offered us unstinting support, guidance and encouragement throughout the process of writing the book and we are most grateful to her for helping us to bring the project to fruition.

ROBERT BOR
ANNE STOKES

About the Authors

Robert Bor is Professor of Psychology and Consultant Clinical Psychologist in the Medical Specialities Directorate at the Royal Free Hospital, London. He is a Chartered Clinical, Counselling and Health Psychologist registered with the Health Professions Council, a Chartered Scientist, as well as a Fellow of the British Psychological Society. He is also a UKCP Registered Family Therapist. He completed his specialist systemic family therapy training at the Tavistock Clinic, London, and is a clinical member of the Institute of Family Therapy, London, and a member of the UK Association for Family Therapy, the American Association for Marital and Family Therapy, the American Psychological Association and the American Family Therapy Academy. Outside of the NHS, Rob runs a successful private practice in the UK and abroad, Dynamic Change Consultants Ltd (www.dccclinical.com). He is also an executive coach and provides services to private and public sector leaders. He works with individuals, couples and families using cognitive behavioural and systemic therapies within a time-limited framework. Rob consults to St Paul's School, the Royal Ballet School and JFS. He also consults to the London Oncology Clinic as well as the London Clinic, both in Harley Street. He is an aviation clinical psychologist with expertise in passenger and crew behaviour and consults to British Airways and the Royal Air Force. He is a past recipient of the BPS Division of Counselling Psychology Award for Outstanding Scientific Achievement. Rob is a Churchill Fellow. He has published more than 25 books and 150 academic papers in peer review journals. He serves on the editorial board of numerous academic journals.

Anne Stokes is a Senior BACP accredited counsellor, trainer and supervisor. She obtained her Diploma in Counselling from the University of Reading, and an MSc in Counselling Training and Supervision from the University of Bristol. Previously Anne worked in secondary education, latterly as deputy head of an 11–18 comprehensive, when she obtained her masters in business administration. Alongside counselling and supervision, Anne has developed other aspects of her independent practice including coaching, mentoring and outplacement consultancy. As a part-time lecturer at the University of Bristol, she led the Diploma in Counselling at Work, and the MSc in Counselling Training and Supervision. Anne runs a variety of courses for commercial, education and charitable organizations. A more recent development has been her interest in online therapy, where, as a Director of Counselling Online Ltd, she trains counsellors to work online, and maintains an independent online counselling and supervision practice. Anne has published a number of chapters and articles, as well as co-authoring another book in this Palgrave Macmillan series.

Chapter 1

Introduction

Working in private, independent practice is no easy option when compared to regular paid employment. The challenges and risks are in fact arguably greater. The skills required to be successful are considerably broader and are not taught as part of one's training. Fortunes can change rapidly and unexpectedly. There is no 'buffer' between you and your client: no institution to hide behind or within and no colleagues at your side from whom to have social and professional support when needed. Working in independent practice will expose all of your strengths as a practitioner, as well as any weaknesses. Independent practice can be isolating and leave us feeling more vulnerable in terms of our confidence as practitioners.

As you read the paragraph above, you might well be thinking 'If it's that bad, I don't think I'll bother.' However, there is another side to working in independent practice and, as one person has said to us, 'The only impact has been favourable, and managing my own time is so freeing.'

Throughout the chapters in this book, we will inevitably look at the problems involved, in the belief that forewarned is forearmed, but we hope you will also gain a sense of the real satisfaction that comes from working in this context.

When we set out to write this book, we had in mind therapists who are just beginning to work independently. However, as time has gone on, we have recognized that we are also writing for experienced practitioners, including ourselves! The reflection on what is required to maintain a professional and ethical independent practice has made us re-evaluate our own work, and in some cases, go back to doing things that have fallen by the wayside, and in others update ourselves in order to be in line with current thinking. We are no different from our colleagues, and if we 'knew then what we know now' we would probably have grown our practices less haphazardly, with less flying by the seat of our pants. So we hope that if you are already working in independent practice, you will still find this book of use to you. At the end of this chapter, we have included a conversation between some independent practitioners.

THE IMPETUS BEHIND THE GROWTH IN INDEPENDENT PRACTICE

Psychologists have historically enjoyed better work options due to their being employed within the NHS, although a sizable number of counsellors and therapists are now working in primary care settings. Some counsellors and therapists have encountered hardships relating to employability and job stability. The economic situation has led to a reduction in the number of jobs available in the NHS and other public service organizations. Many counsellors and therapists, however, have had no option but to work in independent practice. Changes in the NHS, the credit crunch, and what may be arguably an oversupply of qualified therapists relative to salaried jobs mean that more and more practitioners are turning to working independently, even if on a part-time basis.

There are increasingly constraints in working practices in some organizations that may affect enjoyment and satisfaction with your therapy practice. These include the increasing dominance of specific approaches and models within therapy, which can impose limits on the methods and skills that some practitioners can use in practice. Third party organizations such as employee assistance programmes (EAPs) and medical insurers may impose limits on the number of sessions that they will sanction for their clients, which may influence practitioners' models, goals and therapeutic methods.

An absence of reward for loyalty in organizations, as well as clinical and organizational needs (e.g. Agenda for Change in the NHS), may encourage or propel some practitioners to work in the independent sector. The prospects for promotion may also be changing, making it more difficult for practitioners to progress up the career ladder to more senior positions. Practitioners may be required to work outside of those areas in which they originally trained. However, more positively, therapists are employed in many large organizations and their skills are increasingly valued in diverse settings. This makes it more possible for them to work outside of those organizations traditionally associated with the provision of counselling and psychotherapy, such as the NHS.

There is some mystique about developing an independent practice in counselling and psychotherapy. The nature, organization and range of different practices that have been set up vary widely with regard to the fee structures, the therapeutic approaches offered and the management of different practices. There are also strongly held beliefs among some professional colleagues as to who should work in private independent practice. For example, some colleagues feel that this context is unsuited to a practitioner who has only recently qualified. In theory we might agree with that; it is useful to gain experience before striking out on your own. In practice, this may be an out of date and idealistic concept. As several newly qualified counsellors have told us, they actually need to earn after spending time and money on their training. If there are no paid posts available, or they are only available to experienced counsellors, they may consider independent practice running alongside a placement in an organization as a way forward.

Some people are successful in business generally and in independent practice specifically. Others unfortunately are not. This book aims to address some of the challenges, opportunities and skills necessary for setting up and running a successful independent practice in counselling and psychotherapy. It is not intended to be prescriptive and each practitioner will have to make their own decisions about marketing, fee structure, consulting rooms, managing their finances, organizing secretarial services, as well as many other facets that are relevant to running an independent practice. This is but one version of independent practice. You need to create your own version.

Just as each client has a unique account of their problems and/or distress and what has brought them to seek therapy, so too each therapist who intends working in independent practice will need to address for themselves their motivation for this context and type of work and be willing to reflect on their preparedness for it. As you will see in this book, having good psychotherapeutic skills is only one element in ensuring your success as an independent practitioner.

When we asked practitioners for their motivation, we had a variety of answers, as you might expect. Some of these were:

- I was tired of being involved in the politics of organizations.
- I had been a successful manager at work and thought I could use those skills in my counselling practice.
- I wanted to be free to arrange my own diary . . . and life!
- It gave me more opportunity to see a range of clients and issues.
- I wanted to work with both long- and short-term clients – when I was employed, there was pressure to keep to six sessions with everyone.

■ A GP asked me to see one of his patients privately, and it kind of grew from there – I realized I could do it, and I liked doing it!

■ I'm the kind of person who likes new challenges, so decided this was the next step for me.

These and other motivations will be looked at again in later chapters, but give a flavour of why people want to have their own practice.

It is surprising that there are few courses on setting up and developing an independent practice in counselling and psychotherapy. We are aware of only a small handful of courses that include a short presentation on this topic. It is therefore left to qualified professionals to discover for themselves how to develop their practice, and much of this must be attributed to trial and error and also to learning about the experience of others.

For us, this is hardly a satisfactory way in which to encourage more practitioners to work independently, or to teach or share the skills that are necessary in order to ensure a greater chance of success. It is in everyone's interest, including that of professional colleagues as well as aspirant clients, that the independent counselling and psychotherapy sector thrives. It is important that clients have choices available to them so that they can select whom they wish to consult, when and where sessions would best suit their schedule and lifestyle, and also have choices in the amount of counselling or therapy that they wish to undergo. So, that tells you something about *our* motivation for writing this book!

There are three routes or contexts in which a qualified practitioner might develop their independent practice.

1. *Ad hoc.* It could be an add-on to one's main, salaried employment and in this sense is an ad hoc or occasional independent practice service. Many practitioners nowadays are not employed full-time in salaried jobs. Looking to the future, they may wish to augment their livelihood or take on private clients because they may feel that this is a less constraining context in which to practise.

2. *Portfolio.* A second context for practice is again alongside salaried employment, but where independent practice is a part of a portfolio of different work activities that the practitioner enjoys. For example, this may include working in the NHS part-time, working in a GP surgery part-time, working for an EAP and, perhaps alongside this, teaching in a college or university. In this context, similar to that above, the practitioner purposefully chooses a range of different work settings in which to develop their practice and enhance their skills.

3. *Primary*. Some practitioners only work in independent practice and this is on either a full- or a part-time basis. This is therefore their primary, if not exclusive, work context.

Your choice of work context will depend on a number of factors. These include:

■ your interests;
■ pragmatic reasons such as availability of independently funded clients;
■ the stage of your professional development;
■ trigger events such as referrals to see clients privately;
■ the capacity and motivation to run a business in some form.

As we said above, necessity may also be a reason; there will always be therapists who are trained and motivated but for whom there are no salaried jobs.

YOUR PROFESSIONAL IDENTITY OR 'TAG'

There are numerous different titles to the different professions who work psychotherapeutically:

■ Psychologist, psychotherapist and counsellor.
■ In addition, there are some specialist titles, such as child psychotherapist, family therapist, group therapist, as well as psychoanalyst.
■ There are also specialist titles typically used by people who have advanced qualifications and a professional registration in one of the approaches to therapy. For example, some practitioners are specialist cognitive behaviour therapists, rational emotive therapists or brief therapists, among many others.
■ There is also the emerging specialism of life or business coaching, whether this is in the commercial sector or for individual clients.

This book does not distinguish between these different groups as there is considerable overlap between them. It would also need a much longer book in order to address some of the specific issues that relate to each of these. Nonetheless, we have tried to describe what is common to independent practice for all of these professional groups, although we are aware that each of them may engender different approaches to clinical practice, relating to clients, expectations of what happens in client sessions (including the duration of sessions, length and course of therapy etc.) and differing fee structures.

For this reason, working in independent practice does not involve just one specific set of skills or guidelines that each practitioner should follow. These will need to be carefully considered in the light of your unique training, theoretical model(s) used, geographical location and 'case law' of how other colleagues practise in your area, as well as other considerations.

Below, we have included part of a conversation with some counsellors who were in the process of starting their own practice. It is not the whole conversation, and some more of it will be picked up later in the book. We hope it will begin to illustrate some of the points we have made above.

A Conversation with Some Counsellors Setting up in Independent Practice

Anne: So I am wondering if you can tell me a little about the reasons for setting up your own practice. What are the motivating factors for you?

Belinda: Well I have worked part time in a paid post for some time now, and I feel that I've got enough experience to set up on my own. I'm going to do it alongside my paid post to start with, but I hope that if all goes well, eventually I'll be completely independent.

Anne: Have you always had that as your goal?

Belinda: No; when I first started out as a counsellor, I couldn't imagine ever working in my own practice.

Carole: Yes, I felt the same. Being independent seemed something that was really 'grown up' and only counsellors who were very, very experienced and 'old' would do. And that's nonsense really, as I knew several counsellors who had gone that route after a couple of years' experience, but somehow, that didn't sink in.

Anne: So for both of you, it was important to have some experience working in a paid post first?

Carole: I haven't been paid; I have been in a voluntary organization. But I needed to be part of a team and have the backup if I felt uncertain.

David: It's interesting listening to you, as I have only recently finished my degree. So I have been in a placement (well several,

⚏➡

in fact) during those years. Now I need to earn some money, partly because I have paid out so much for training, and partly because our family budget needs it. I can't find a paid job, and so I have set up my practice.

Anne: Would you have preferred to be in a paid post?

David: At first, I thought that I would, and that being self-employed was second best, because I couldn't find anything. However, now I am excited by the whole thing, and really want to do it for its own sake.

Belinda: Aren't you worried that people will ask you how long you've been doing this, and what it will feel like to say that you are newly qualified?

David: A bit; but then I remind myself that when I was training and in a placement, no one ever asked how long I'd been counselling, and they didn't know who was a trainee and who was qualified. So maybe no client will ask now!

Carole: Good point. No one has ever asked me either.

Belinda: But I'm wondering if it's OK to go into private work straight after qualifying.

David: Sounds as if you are saying it isn't?

Belinda: I am not sure. I think it's like Carole was saying, there needs to be backup from a team when we start out.

David: I can see that would be good, but it is possible to get round that, as I haven't that luxury.

Anne: Can you tell us the ways you're getting round that?

David: Yes. I have joined a group of people who are in private practice. Most of them are more experienced than me, so I can lean on them a bit. Then I've chosen a supervisor who is experienced in her own practice and who is willing to support me in mine. I'm also in group supervision with him, as well as one to one, so I can make contacts there. Obviously money is tight at present, but I've joined a counselling organization that provides talks and workshops at very low costs (I think they only aim to cover their expenses) so I can get CPD and a network there. Lastly, I have talked to a GP and a psychiatrist that I know, and both have said that they don't mind me contacting them occasionally if I need to for information and professional advice.

Anne: Wow! You've really thought this through well. It sounds great.

Belinda: You are making me think about some things that would be sensible for me to do as well, even though I will still have my team for a bit.

Carole: Yes, thanks. Maybe there is something useful about initially being forced into this way of working that makes you really think it through.

David: I think that's possibly right. I can't afford for this not to work in the long term – I know it will still take time to build up.

Ellie: I have been sitting here listening to you all. It's quite the opposite for me. As you know, when I left work to have the baby, I thought it would be a good opportunity to think about starting my own practice when he was a little bit older. Now I know that I don't want to do that. I do need professional contact with adults other than clients. I need to be in a team. So I am now thinking that I will find paid work if I can for about one day a week. In time, I may go back to the idea of also doing some private work, but for now, one day a week is all the time I want to be away from him, so I don't miss stages of his development. I don't want someone else to be the first to see him doing things – I want to be there!

Carole: That sounds good to me. Both about the baby and you, but also that you've made a choice *not* to work on your own. If we're going to work independently, it has to be something we feel passionate about and ready to commit to, in my opinion.

CONCLUSION

We hope that the ideas in this book will help you to develop a successful practice and avoid difficulties or even failure. You will discover that there is some overlap between chapters as we consider issues from different angles. As most therapists do in their professional work, reflection on therapeutic process helps us to clarify our thoughts and goals. Before reading on, you might like to consider some of the questions below that may be relevant to reflecting on your interest in developing an independent therapy practice.

Reflexive Points

- What are my motivations for working independently?
- Why am I thinking about or planning this at this stage of my career?
- What experiences qualify me to work independently?
- What might I miss out on professionally working in independent practice?
- What could I stand to gain professionally and personally?
- What is the likely impact on my friends, family and loved ones?

Chapter 2

Advantages and Disadvantages of Independent Practice

INTRODUCTION

In Chapter 1, we touched on the reasons why you might want to work independently. Here we look in more detail at types of independent practice, the advantages and disadvantages, some of the stressors and finally whether it is right for you.

The success or failure of your new venture may depend largely on your initial attitude to beginning the venture. If you are seeing it as second best to being fully employed, it is possible that your preconceptions will influence how you develop it. You may skip over the necessary steps and find yourself with a low number of clients, and a sense of dissatisfaction.

If, on the other hand, it is something you embrace and give the time to researching it and developing it fully, you stand to gain both financially and emotionally. So take time to think about whether you really want to choose this path – you must have had some initial pull towards it, or you wouldn't be reading this book! As one practitioner we know said, 'There are times when I am fed up with doing my accounts, overtired and frustrated that I have to pay all my own costs, yet when I get up in the morning, I look forward to being mistress of my day. I have chosen to work with these clients, and they have chosen to work with me. I have choices, which feels liberating.'

You may already be working independently, so may wish to move on through the book. However, it can still be useful to remember what it was that made you make the choice. 'Perhaps it is worth reflecting on this important career change that has the potential to bring excitement, hard work and challenge. For some counsellors, it also triggers anxiety' (McMahon et al., 2005). It is easy to think that much of what we have written below is obvious, but often we overlook it! So here we encourage you to think about how it applies to you and your situation. Over a decade ago, Anderson (1998) said that a key skill is not about managing change, but about managing surprises. That is certainly still true today in independent practice.

TYPES OF INDEPENDENT PRACTICE

Independent practice can operate in various ways. It may run alongside paid employment, which is either full- or part-time. You can become a partner in an existing independent practice, or form one with other practitioners you already know, and whose work and business acumen you respect. You can also become a limited company, though unless your turnover is high enough to need to do this, you will need to weigh up the advantages against the disadvantages.

Practitioners may be self-employed, but see only clients referred to them through other organizations, such as:

- GP practices;
- primary health trusts;
- employee assistance programmes;
- occupational health and human relations departments;
- injury or health insurance companies.

In addition, clients may be self-referring.

WHY CHOOSE THIS WAY OF WORKING?

Practitioners come to it for different reasons. For counsellors and psychotherapists, it may be as simple as the fact that it is difficult to find full-time employed work. So it may be an adjunct to a part-time post, or because of the awareness that, having trained, if you don't want to remain counselling solely on a voluntary basis, you need to set up in independent practice.

Psychologists and psychiatrists are more generally employed after their initial training and come to independent practice at a later stage of their career. It may be that they wish to pursue a particular specialism, or that they wish to be more able to choose their clients and their working context. Often they will begin by (and may choose to remain) working partly in an employed capacity and partly independently.

Many of us have friends and colleagues who are in independent practice, and listening to their narratives may motivate us to take the risk of branching out on our own. We may simply have the desire or the need to do something different. Perhaps we are tired of the predictability of our current role, or are aware of changes taking place, and decide to move on before our organization alters or disbands.

For some now well established practitioners, it has been purely a serendipitous happening. Someone asked us to see a client privately while in paid employment. We did this, and found that other requests follow, so took the decision to start our own practice. In fact, doing a quick trawl of our colleagues and contacts, most of them said that this was how they had begun!

> One established therapist said to us: 'I think that although it may be how lots of us got started, it was all a bit hit and miss. I am talking about twelve years ago, and I do think it was easier then. People starting now are expected to be much more professional and businesslike. That's what clients and referrers expect.'

Certainly, for all practitioners, if you can have the luxury of being in some paid employment as you develop your own practice, this can help to cushion you financially. However, that division can also bring some tensions, such as how you split your time, and possible conflicts of interest.

ADVANTAGES OF WORKING INDEPENDENTLY

More freedom

There is a sense of freedom in being able to choose how and when you work. You can arrange your working life around your lifestyle and the other calls on your time, such as carer roles. If you are working from home, you dispense with the daily commute and can make use of the gaps in between clients to do other things not connected with your work, without the nagging sense that you should be focused on work tasks. Above all, you are accountable only to yourself (and of course, your client and your professional organization).

Many practitioners find satisfaction in being able to see clients who are not able to get referrals through the NHS or their workplace well-being schemes. Even those who could be referred for funded treatment may choose to come to you rather than be put on a long waiting list. This may mean that they engage in treatment at an earlier point, when the outcome is likely to be more successful or quicker than if they had waited. This feedback from a client bears this out:

> When I came to you, I was a bit resentful that I had to pay. I could have waited and seen someone for free through my GP. However, there was a six month waiting list, and I needed to work out what to do now. If I had waited, I think that events would have over-taken me, and I'd have been in a much worse place.

Choices in arranging the diary

In independent practice, there is a choice in the number of clients you take on. So rather than seeing people on the hour, every hour, you can work out what enables you to practise most effectively, and with the most fulfilment. There is more flexibility in arranging sessions for a particular client when you manage your own diary. So, for example, an independent practitioner can often more easily accommodate a client who works shifts than one who is working set hours in an organization, particularly if it only operates a standard working day. It is also easier to negotiate changes to usual client hours if you wish to attend a CPD event or a meeting, for example. You have greater 'give' in your diary to offer an alternative time, rather than have to cancel a client's session. This of course would not be acceptable if your particular theoretical approach would see such a change of time or day as a breach of the therapeutic relationship.

Monetary choices

There are also choices in your fee structures. At least on paper, you will be receiving more per hour than if employed. You can also choose to negotiate fees with clients who cannot afford full fees – these choices are yours rather than imposed upon you by the policies and structures of umbrella organizations. We look at fees in greater depth in a later chapter.

Attendance rates

Hudson-Allez (2007) posits another advantage. She suggests that attendance rates are higher in the independent sector. If clients are paying for their own therapy, then they are likely to turn up for sessions. There is a greater personal investment in the process. Hudon-Allez gives the non-attendance rates in primary care as between 10 and 25 per cent. This would be financially disastrous in private practice. From our own experience, few of our clients in our independent work do not attend or cancel, except for genuine reasons such as emergencies and illness. Our rate would be something like 2 to 5 per cent.

Choices in evaluation methods

You will need to think how you monitor and evaluate your own practice (there is more about how to do this elsewhere in the book). For some people this is a huge advantage as they can devise ways of doing this that give them the information they feel is most relevant for their individual practice. For others, this could be a disadvantage as they have been used to, and prefer, standardized forms such as CORE. This is an expensive choice, though beginning to be used by independent practitioners who wish feedback from an external source. There can also be something reassuring about using a standard form: 'If it's official, it must be better than mine!' said one colleague.

Specialism – or not

Another advantage is that you can choose to specialize in a particular area – for example, working with adolescents, or couples. Conversely, if you have worked in an organization or department that offers a specialism, independent practice allows you to develop your skills and interests with a wider range of clients.

Using your other skills

You may have a range of skills that fit better into independent practice than paid employment – for example, in some of these areas of private work:

■ coaching and mentoring practice;
■ for psychologists and psychiatrists in particular, undertaking independent assessments or legal reports, as well as expert witness work;
■ teaching on established courses;
■ developing your own courses or workshops, which is more possible when you are not tied into a regular salaried post;

- supervision of other practitioners (employed and self-employed) if you have the necessary experience and training;
- consultancy;
- media work.

Below we look at two other areas to consider.

Expert witness

One specialist, niche area of independent practice for a therapist to move into either as their main work or in addition to other professional activity is as an expert witness. An expert witness is, by definition, a professional whose expertise, experience and ability to be fair and impartial are especially valued in contentious situations. Almost all expert witness work is of court standard, meaning that reports or evidence must be acceptable within a legal context. It can, but does not necessarily, entail being a witness in court and providing evidence that may need to be explained and defended under cross examination. It is therefore not a specialism to be taken lightly, as you can hear from this quote from a colleague:

> I could not possibly have done this when I was starting out as an independent practitioner. It's not that I didn't have the expertise or knowledge. I had that. It's more about having the support and team behind you to come back and talk to. I needed to have my personal professional network in place before I was confident enough to do this on my own.

There are no formal criteria for becoming an expert witness. It is more likely to be a position or role that evolves and develops from your work. An expert witness is likely to:

- have gained a positive reputation in their specialist field;
- have experience preparing court-level reports about clients, problems or specific topics;
- be able confidently and fairly to appraise situations and defend their views;
- demonstrate good analytical skills.

Employee assistance programmes (EAPs)

Therapists who work for EAPs are mostly associates who undertake time-limited therapy and are contracted by the provider rather than directly by the client. The EAP will have formed a contract with business and organizations to provide counselling services for its employees. The work typically involves offering between four and eight telephone or face-to-face sessions to employees of a company, often at relatively short notice.

The advantage for the therapist is that you receive referrals from a support health care organization, although the fact that there is some prescription over the therapy approaches and the number of sessions available may not appeal to all therapists.

Following your own ways of doing things

Although you will need to develop your own contracts, policies and procedures for all your independent work, they will be *yours*. They will fit your values and assumptions about working therapeutically, rather than being imposed on you. This may also apply to your consulting room. You can choose the colour scheme, the chairs, the pictures, the objects in it. Obviously if you rent premises, some of these will be 'givens', but generally there is more choice.

Pacing yourself

Working in independent practice can be surprisingly tiring, so you need to have stamina, particularly if you are entering the later years of your working life. This may sound like a disadvantage, but in fact if you choose to work at a pace that suits you, it is an excellent way of working fewer hours than in paid employment. For some people, it can even be a way of easing into retirement, though there are many independent practitioners who enjoy working well past normal retirement age, even if they simply work a few hours a week. One of us in this bracket now, and is enjoying the luxury of being able to slowly reduce working time as and when she feels ready to do so.

In summing up the advantages, the key word to emerge is 'choice'. One of the reasons most frequently given when independent practitioners are asked why they work this way is that 'it allows me to be my own master/mistress and make my own choices and decisions'.

WHAT ARE THE DISADVANTAGES?

Sadly, independent practice is not a complete bed of roses. There are disadvantages as well as advantages. For that reason, in the remaining chapters, we will look at how you might make your practice as viable as possible.

Lack of security

The most obvious disadvantage is that there is no predictable flow of income. As you start up your practice, the number of clients can be disconcertingly low, even though you have taken time to plan your strategies. Even in well established practices, client numbers can fluctuate greatly due to factors outside your control such as the summer holiday period or a recession. Time you take away from your practice, for holidays, for example, is unpaid time, and needs to be considered when you are setting your budget and fee structure.

Add-on costs

There are also add-on costs, such as personal pension plans, professional indemnity, National Insurance, health insurance that will pay out if you are unable to work, conferences or CPD workshop fees, supervision fees, advertising and possibly renting premises. You may need an accountant, and don't forget the apparently trivial items such as stamps, stationery and cartridges for your computer printer. All of these things mount up, as one practitioner told us.

> The first month when I added up my costs, I was horrified! I seemed to have spent all my income. It did get better, and I learned not to panic.

What is your real income?

As mentioned in the advantages, you will probably be paid more per hour than if employed. However, this is on paper! There will be hours when you aren't paid. These may be client slots that are not currently filled, or the hours when you have to attend to the administration of your practice. Do not underestimate the time needed to attend to administration – if you hate it while you are employed, that is not going to change when you are self-employed. Apart from client notes, you will also need to keep full and accurate records of income and expenditure for tax purposes. Time will also be needed for marketing yourself, and developing good networks for referrals. For every client hour, you need to add in administration time too, possibly as much as half as much again.

Isolation

Another disadvantage may be a sense of isolation. Much of your time will be spent on your own or with clients. If you are used to meeting and chatting with colleagues about professional matters and also more social conversations, it can feel a stark contrast when you are working by yourself, with no casual meetings over coffee or in the corridors. You need to be fairly resilient and self-sufficient to work in independent practice, and to build in professional contacts.

Irregular hours

Hours can be irregular. While this *can* work to your advantage, if you prefer 'set hours' then working at times that suit clients can be difficult. Clients may want early morning, lunchtime, evening or Saturday appointments, so you can find you have gaps in your day, or are working when friends and family are not. Once you are well established, you may be able to regulate this, but initially you probably have to take clients when it is convenient for them and not the other way round.

Consulting rooms

Your consulting room may throw up disadvantages. If you are very lucky, you may be able to rent by the hour, but many rooms understandably are let for blocks of time. If you are working from home, and have a family, the disruption to them has to be considered. Will they be happy having to maintain a low profile while you have clients? Have you got a consulting room that is not used for other purposes? Can clients access a toilet without going into the main part of your house? Will friends and neighbours (or the postman or electricity meter reader!) respect the fact that when you are working, you are absolutely not available?

> Just recently a supervisee said, 'I thought I'd got all this stuff sussed. Family sorted; dog under control; nice room. Then I started working with couples, and my room was just not big enough. I had the choice of the three of us being squashed, or moving the family out of another room, and taking all the personal stuff out, every time I saw a couple. In the end, I rented a friend's counselling room one evening a week, and only saw couples there.'

It's harder to be a blank screen

If you do choose to work from home, it is inevitable that your client will know more about you than if you work within rented property or in an organization's premises. They can see what type of neighbourhood you live in, perhaps what car you drive, be able to see into other parts of the house as they approach your door, or see evidence of your family, such as a child's bike on the drive. The furnishings have a more personal meaning as they are 'yours' and not the institution's.

For some practitioners, this may be of no consequence or something that can be used in the therapeutic process. Field (2007) has an interesting section on dealing therapeutically with the envy that might be inspired by working from home. However, for those of a more analytical approach, who want to remain as unknown as possible in order for the work to take place, working from home would be a huge disadvantage. As Field says, 'The very nature of working from home introduces a new context to the therapeutic work and creates dynamics peculiar to it.'

Are some clients going to be excluded?

Depending on where you live or rent accommodation, you may exclude certain client groups. For example, if you live in a village, bus times may be problematic, and therefore you exclude anyone who cannot drive, or be driven, to you. Certain areas in a town where you live or rent may seem too upmarket for some clients, or conversely appear to be in 'dodgy' neighbourhoods.

No institutional buffer

If you work in an organization, you have what Symes (1994) describes as 'an institutional buffer'. In other words, you have the weight of the organization behind you in matters related to codes of practice, client allocation, short- or long-term counselling contracts, contents of contracts, policies and whether there is a fee structure or not. An independent practitioner does not have this backing, but has to make their own decisions, and carry the total responsibility for them. In addition, you need to have an understanding of the law and legal implications. While this is true for all practitioners, those in independent practice need to be aware that 'the actual application of the law may vary according to the employment context of the individual therapist i.e. whether the therapist is working as self employed or employed by an organisation, and according to the setting, such as working for a statutory agency, or in a private practice' (Jenkins, 2002).

Security

Another advantage of working in an organization is that generally you do not have to consider your own security arrangements, other than at a fairly minimal level. This is very different in independent practice, where there may not be anyone else around in the building, particularly if you are working from your home. While in reality your personal safety is rarely at risk, the disadvantage of this aspect of independent practice should never be ignored. Several practitioners told us that when they saw clients for the first time, they always made sure that it was obvious that someone else was around.

This section on the disadvantages of working independently might seem gloomy and depressing. However, it is better to know what you are taking on than to find out later. Our experience shows that despite the drawbacks, most independent practitioners thoroughly enjoy their work, and are skilful in turning problems into solutions!

STRESS AND STRESSORS

While, notionally, practitioners know a great deal about stress and regularly deal with this as an issue in their clients, often they disregard it as something that will affect them when they set up in private practice. They know the theory, and they have survived stressful situations when employed, so they reason that they can cope with it in independent practice. So what are the stressors?

Finance

The financial impact and the time it takes to build up an independent practice are obvious ones, though perhaps because they are obvious, practitioners are better prepared for them and have thought through strategies to deal with them before embarking on the new venture. Money has been put aside to ease the initial months of low income, or the decision has been made to stay in part-time work (whether in the therapeutic world, or in a previous career) until client numbers build up. If necessary, talk to your bank about their means of supporting new businesses.

No network

Before embarking, it is wise to talk to other independent practitioners, not just about the practicalities of working this way, but about what they have found stressful, and how they have dealt with it. Build up a network of useful professionals very early on, and find yourself a good mentor or supervisor. We mentioned the groups we run with beginning practitioners earlier in the chapter. Here are extracts from some members' e-mails after a recent session:

> It is such a help to meet with you all. I do need the support as I can feel very alone . . .
>
> Wasn't the discussion great? I still totally disagree with X, but it is so good to be able to have that depth of intellectual challenge, so thanks!
>
> I've taken your advice about tackling the printers re that last batch of leaflets, and am having a meeting with their boss on Friday. Will let you know how that goes.

The family

Discuss with family or significant others in your life how you will all cope with the demands. If they have been consulted, and their concerns and ideas for managing taken into account, they are much more likely to support you, and relationships will be less impaired.

When there's no work

How will you manage times when you are not working, but would like to be? They can be used for a mixture of developing the business, and using the opportunity for other things that you have previously wanted to do, but haven't found the time. This will vary widely with individuals – taking exercise, improving your IT abilities, reading, gardening or learning a new skill are all possibilities. It is probably not wise to join a class or a group that meets at specific times, as you may find that you add stress by deciding whether to go to there or see a potential referral.

Running a business

If the practical side of running a business feels daunting, research your local adult education centres for courses for new ventures. These are often free or low cost, and may be flexible in terms of when you need to attend. As well as being useful sources of information, they give you the opportunity of sharing concerns with like-minded people. They may not be in the same line of work, but there will be similar stresses.

Administration

In addition, keep on top of the administration. It is extremely stressful to be faced with an enormous pile of paperwork, stretching back over weeks or months. Financial records are best kept up to date regularly, so that you don't have to wade through piles of cheque stubs, receipts and credit card statements, or go back through your diary to work out what your mileage is for legitimate claims on the business accounts. The end of the tax year is not the ideal time to do a year's worth of accounts. It sounds so obvious, but the reality is that few independent practitioners have had to do business records in previous employment, and can get into a muddle by putting things off.

Unrealistic expectations

Travilla (1990) discusses the concept of 'caring without wearing' and lists five unrealistic expectations of caregivers.

■ I have the ability to change another person.
■ I have the capacity to help everyone.
■ There should never be any limits to what I can do.
■ I am the only person available to help.
■ I must never make a mistake.

These apply to well trained, experienced professionals too. While the first two are issues dealt with very early on in our therapeutic training, it is surprisingly easy to forget these basics when in independent practice. We get caught up in wanting to enhance our reputation, so that our clients will recommend us to others. We somehow think we can take on all clients, in our need to fill our client slots, and ignore the fact that we wouldn't normally choose to work with this issue, or that we are not the best person to help this particular individual. Stress follows!

The other unrealistic expectations are also helpful for independent practitioners. An easy trap for us to fall into is to be overavailable to clients or potential clients in ways that we wouldn't consider if we were employed. For example, there is a balance between responding to phone calls promptly and never putting on the answerphone, so that we can enjoy some time when we are not working. We do need time away from work.

Turning clients down

Another stressor is feeling that you must take on a client if they contact you. If you can't fit them in at this time, tell them so, rather than unrealistically juggle your diary. You are not the only person available. Build up your contact list of people you are happy to refer an enquirer to. The fear is that if we don't make ourselves available, we will find we have no clients. However, in our experience, passing potential clients on works both ways. Other practitioners will do the same for you when they have a full caseload.

It may also mean that should you become ill and unable to work, you have a possible set of people to call on. Occasionally independent practitioners work when they might otherwise have taken time off because they are unwell. While this is not to be recommended, it happens sometimes because it seems too stressful to cancel clients, and there are no colleagues to cover appointments, or even to rearrange your appointments.

Not knowing what success means

Before you set out on this road, it is useful to have a definition of what success may mean to you. You might like to pause here in your reading, and take time out to reflect, write or draw what success will look like.

If you decide that you wish to break even within six months, and you do that, it will not increase your stress levels. However, if you decide that you need to be showing a profit, or a reasonable income, within three months and you don't happen to achieve your target, up goes the stress. What is realistic for one person in terms of defining success may be very different from that for someone else. It is up to you to decide your own criteria. Thistle (1998) has an interesting chapter on defining stress in private practice, where he considers a range of possible measures, from keeping clients to considering what has gone wrong.

A 'be perfect' driver

Finally, realistically everyone who has set up their own practice has made some mistakes – hopefully not therapeutic ones! Remember Winnicot, and aim to be 'good enough'. If you tell yourself that you must run your business perfectly, you are going to end up feeling harassed and incompetent. Learn from what goes wrong, rather than dwelling on it.

Not taking care of ourselves

Don't forget the basics. To work well and avoid harmful stress, we need to take care of ourselves. We need professional and personal support and encouragement; proper rest and exercise; to be able to set limits and boundaries; and to have non-work time. There is nothing new or revolutionary in this list. We know it well, but can get so caught up in growing our business that we can ignore these fundamentals, and become burnt out.

CONCLUSION: WILL INDEPENDENT PRACTICE SUIT YOU?

In Chapter 1, we listed some of the assumptions about practising independently. If these apply to you, then professionally, independent practice is an option. There are also some characteristics that may be important to take into consideration. If the answer to most of the questions below is 'yes' then your profile is suited to working this way.

- Am I resilient?
- Am I flexible in my thinking and approach to problems?
- Do I have both creative and logical thinking patterns?
- Can I adapt easily?
- Do I like change?
- Am I resourceful?
- Will I be able to plan and organize my practice without undue stress?
- Do I have good professional and personal support?
- Do I have stamina?
- Can I cope with fluctuating caseloads?
- How am I on taking acceptable risks?
- Do I have any business knowledge or skills? If not, am I prepared to acquire them?
- In addition, most importantly, is this something I really want to do now?

The following chapters will give you much more specific detail about many of the practical and therapeutic issues raised in this chapter.

Before reading on you might wish to think further about the personal pros and cons by working through the questions below.

Reflexive Points

- Will I be happy working alone or do I need to have a colleague?
- What skills do I have that could give me variety in my work?
- Would my close friends and family support my decision?
- Have I got enough financial security to do this?
- What are my stressors and can I manage them?

Finally, if imagery and visualization techniques appeal to you, find a quiet time and space, and undertake a relaxation exercise that works well for you. Then visualize various aspects of your work as an independent practitioner. Work through reflections about setting up or continuing your practice as well as imagining your clients. Notice whether it is a pleasurable or stressful visualization. When you have completed it, you may want to note down the various images and feelings that you had.

Chapter 3

Choosing the Practice Location

INTRODUCTION

All therapists in independent practice need to consider where they will see their clients. This need not be in one specific location and some practitioners choose to work in a number of different settings. The choice of settings may be limited, however, in that financial, practical or other constraints may necessitate working from home. This should not be thought of as a 'second best' as it may be entirely suitable for some clients to see their therapist in the therapist's home, provided it has been suitably adapted for this purpose.

LOCATION

The location of practice rooms is an important practical matter in setting up and developing your practice and has implications for the image and identity that you wish to project. At a practical level, there is the matter of the financial cost to you. In addition, where you see clients will project ideas about how you wish to be viewed by your clients. Some therapists feel that it is important to locate themselves close to other practitioners, such as medical specialists or other counsellors or therapists. An example in London is where some therapists may establish themselves in well known areas such as Harley Street, believing that this conveys something about their stature, reputation and abilities.

While most of us would not be able to afford to do this, an example of how location affects our practice can be seen through Monica's decisions.

Most of the time Monica works at home, but she has occasional referrals from a multinational organization that has its headquarters in the same town. Some of these referrals are at a very senior level, and Monica felt that they might not see her home premises as suitably professional. This may or may not have been true, but it was so in Monica's mind and therefore might have affected how she formed a working alliance with them. She discovered that she could rent an office in a very attractive, centrally located suite of offices by the hour. The rooms had easy chairs and a coffee table, as well as the more formal office furniture. This gives her the setting she wants for these particular clients and does not involve a long-term rental agreement.

While identity may be enhanced by the location of your rooms, do remember that your skills, reputation and professionalism are more important.

ACCESSIBILITY

If your rooms are beautifully furnished but inaccessible, this is likely to be a disincentive to clients to attend. It is usually important that you are close to transport links, or have adequate parking so that clients are able to arrive feeling as little stressed by the journey as possible.

A second aspect of accessibility is how easy it is for clients physically to gain access to your rooms. If it requires finding their way through a large block of flats, or a maze of pedestrian walkways, this could prove challenging and offputting for some.

Others, who have a physical disability, may also find stairs and lengthy corridors a problem. For this reason, ease of access is important and needs to be clearly considered before signing a lease or setting up therapy rooms in your own home environment.

James lives in a small village with poor public transport (though good access to a major motorway). His house also has a very steep drive and a series of steps to reach the front door. Despite the feelings of guilt that this did cause, and still does from time to time, he works very successfully from home, though he is very clear about the access issues when potential clients or referrers contact him.

⫸

He has been challenged when working with clients. For example, he chose to work with a client who has severe mobility problems in the client's own home. This was because the client had difficulties using community-provided disability transport in addition to being wheelchair bound. During the work, there was a protracted period when the client raged against James for not being prepared to spend the money to make his premises wheelchair friendly. It was an extremely hard period during the therapy, because James obviously could not say 'It would cost thousands of pounds to do this and I cannot afford it! And you won't go out to see a therapist anyway'. (Lots of supervision took place, needless to say!) However, therapeutically, it proved to be a turning point in addressing the client's feelings about his disability.

SHARING WITH OTHER THERAPISTS

It may be possible and desirable to share with other therapists who practise in a similar modality or who complement your style of therapeutic practice. The obvious benefit of having colleagues in close proximity is that many of the expenses can be shared. Colleagues may also cross-refer to you if they are either too busy or unavailable for clients who need to see them at a particular time. A disadvantage may be that such colleagues could prove rivals or their reputation may be such that it does little to enhance your own practice. So be careful with whom you decide to share.

There is another possible aspect of sharing that may be worth considering. If you have set up your own therapy room at home, but don't use it all the time, either because you work solely on certain days or because you work away from home on a specific day of the week, you could consider renting the space to a colleague. Obviously if you choose to do this, you need to look at the insurance and tax implications of the venture.

One colleague has told us about how she does this very successfully with someone she did her original training with, and whom she trusts both as a counsellor and as a businessperson. Another has found that it does not work for her for two reasons. The first is that when someone else is using her counselling room, she feels the need to avoid having friends around, and has to ensure that her pets are contained and make no noise. The second is that there was a slight difficulty over a payment by the person renting the room, and our colleague realized that it was hard to combine friendship and business.

SHARING WITH OTHER PROFESSIONALS

This is different to the above in that your colleagues may not be psychotherapeutically trained. In this regard, it may be possible to share with a medical practitioner, dentist, lawyer or other professional who may require similar consultation and office space. For the same reasons listed above, there are both advantages and disadvantages to this. While many clients are used to visiting health centres where there are a number of different types of practitioner, a disadvantage might be that it causes confusion to potential clients who feel that there is a blurring of professional identities.

PROXIMITY TO OTHER THERAPISTS

There are advantages and disadvantages to setting up one's practice close to other counsellors and therapists working in independent practice. A greater number of therapists working in close proximity does not necessarily have clear disadvantages in terms of market share. It is possible in some circumstances for a number of therapists working in a similar locality to provide a 'critical mass' of therapists, which enhances identity and improves marketability of psychotherapeutic services generally. This works best when the therapists have an amicable relationship with one another and potentially diverse therapeutic modalities so that they are not in direct competition with one another. However, a disadvantage is that in some circumstances, it can seem that there are too many therapists 'chasing' too few clients, which means that everyone is disadvantaged.

SUITABILITY OF ROOMS FOR DIFFERENT CLIENT GROUPS

An important consideration is whether your practice will cater for one-to-one sessions with clients only. If you work with couples or families, you may need to have larger rooms and more seating. There are additional issues in terms of safety and suitability if you have the necessary qualifications to work psychotherapeutically with children. Play areas in both your room and waiting area will be necessary, as well as furnishings that can easily be cleaned if you work with sand, water, paints etc.

SAFETY AND SECURITY

It goes without saying that these are of paramount importance in choosing the location and suitability of rooms. Consulting rooms can be easy prey for thieves in that they know that professionals are not present for some of the time. They are likely to have their eye on laptops, cash, computers and other equipment that may be easy to steal from the premises. For this reason, it is wise to have the premises alarmed and to ensure that you have carried out a security assessment.

You may also need to insure your rooms. The space will also need to be safe so that clients are free from any risk of harm. For this reason, a glass coffee table, with sharp edges, and other potentially dangerous objects or furnishings need to be avoided to ensure the safety of clients.

CHEERFULNESS

Most clients wish to consult with a therapist whose rooms reflect either a neutral or cheerful disposition. A gloomy room sends the wrong message! The rooms need to be clean, well maintained, suitably furnished with reasonably comfortable and modern furniture, and be decorated in an agreeable though reasonably neutral way.

PROFESSIONAL APPEARANCE

One of the main difficulties when seeing clients in your own home is how to project a professional appearance when it is clear that it is also where you live. Most therapists would agree that it is important to remove personal items such as family photos, children's toys etc. that could otherwise lead to the client projecting certain ideas or feelings onto you as a consequence of where they see you.

CHOICE OF FURNISHINGS

This is obviously an individual matter. However, to an extent it may reflect your therapeutic modality of practice. Some therapists will want a couch, whereas others will want comfortable armchairs or a sofa where a couple or family can spread themselves out. It is useful to allocate a seat for yourself and often therapists will steer their clients towards where they think they should sit and clients will look to the therapist accordingly. Given that you are responsible for the space, it is important that you provide this level of guidance. Of course, some therapists would see the choice of seating as revealing important aspects of themselves, but if you do not give any guidance, you may find that you end up away from your diary and your glasses, and the client ends up away from the tissues and the bin for throwing them into.

SPECIAL ISSUES WHEN WORKING FROM HOME

There are some obvious differences in seeing clients at home and they are worth careful consideration before you decide to do this. The first is that you need to ensure relative privacy so that your family and neighbours do not come to intrude on your sessions. This is often easier said than done, but may directly affect when you are available to see your clients. You also need to manage the timings between client sessions carefully because unless you have an area in which clients who arrive early can wait, it is best to leave extra time between client sessions so that the flow of clients can be managed accordingly.

Many people have pets and some clients may find it annoying or intrusive to have to pet the dog or listen to a parrot squawking in the background. One enquiry that one of us had was accompanied by a very terse answerphone message: 'If you have cats, I don't want to come to see you as I hate them.'

It is hard to control the neighbour's cats, even if you do managed to train yours (or more probably ensure that there is no way they can be in that space, as cats have minds of their own!) Such things may be a determining feature as to why you can indeed see clients from your own home.

Clients will naturally project ideas, beliefs and feelings onto us about the kind of person we are, based on the physical environment that they encounter. Messy rooms, wandering or noisy pets and personal artefacts may give more information about you than you wish to convey to clients. It is a good idea to invite a friend or colleague into your home to give their impressions of your 'work' environment. It may be that you are so familiar with your home that you fail to see what someone else can spot that will obviously give the wrong impression.

There may be a clear effect on your family life and sessions need to be arranged such that family members and telephone calls do not come to intrude on sessions. Ensuring confidentiality and privacy is of the utmost importance. An important further consideration is the use of toilet facilities. If clients have to walk the length of your home in order to access the toilet, this requires that most other rooms they walk past have to be kept clean, neat and tidy, or the doors must be closed at all times. If the toilet is close to the consulting area, this will reduce the amount of effort you will need to go to in order to ensure the needs of clients are met in this regard. It is also important that the bathroom is kept tidy and clean, as well as ensuring that personal objects such as toothbrushes, perfumes, medications etc. are kept out of view.

CONCLUSION

There are many aspects to choosing a location, and perhaps the main point to stress in conclusion is that there is not one right way to do this. It is important that your choices match your way of working, your finances and your personal preferences. These preferences may include aspects of time management and the following chapter focuses on this.

There are some questions below that may help you think about the key points from this chapter.

Reflexive Points
■ Where will I see clients?
■ Are the premises suited to this or do they have to be adapted?
■ Are my insurances relevant and up to date?
■ Can clients easily access my rooms?
■ Do I have a friend or colleague who would look at my room as if they were a client?

Chapter 4

Managing Your Time

INTRODUCTION

Time management and deciding where you will see your clients are linked, as your practice will almost inevitably consume more of your time than you may feel that you have available. Administration can also deflect from your client practice time, which is the only activity in independent practice by which you earn your living! Private practitioners cannot claim, and do not earn, money while they organize their finances, plan their practices, develop marketing strategies and the like. Therefore, while planning and developing your practice is crucial, this cannot come to dominate over client contact time. If you cannot do some of this administration in the place that you practise, in gaps or when there is a non-attendance, it will add to the burden.

A common challenge for most practitioners who are in the process of developing their independent practice is to find that their day is constantly interrupted by enquiries, paperwork and ad hoc tasks, all of which leave little time to spend on the other vital tasks of planning and conducting their practice. There has to be a balance between keeping the administrative tasks up to date and actually seeing clients.

Very often, it is impossible to delegate these tasks to other people. Unless you are in the fortunate but rare position of being able to employ an administrator or secretary, most of the other tasks will need to be carried out by you. Some, such as clinical notes, cannot be done by anyone else. While you may be very used to doing these in paid employment, there you are not doing them in addition to all the other things.

For this reason, you may need to allocate time to do your banking, maintain clinical records, ensure client letters and referral correspondence is attended to, as well as manage your own personal life. Not all of these things happen every day, but most of them are regular activities.

THINK WHAT WE CAN LEARN FROM BIG BUSINESS

It may seem crass and totally irrelevant to compare running an independent therapy practice to managing an airline. There are, however, some issues that are common to both. Most of us have booked airline tickets for our holidays or professional reasons, so let's think about the issues in common. Airlines sell seats. Like other service sector organizations such as hotels and leisure cruise liners, unsold spaces can never be recovered once the voyage has begun. So once that opportunity has passed and the space has not been sold at whatever price, the owners face some loss of potential revenue.

In therapy, there is a similar process and the potential for the identical loss. We sell our time and skills. If these are not taken up, they cannot later be recovered. A spare therapeutic hour when we intended to be working has the same consequence as a half empty aircraft – no income.

There are some differences, of course. As one rather angry colleague said on reading this, 'So you are saying that my practice will be all about bums on seats?' The answer must clearly be 'No, not at all. Unlike an airline, we need to get the right bums on seats if we are to succeed ethically. Though if we don't get some bums there at all, we will surely fail.'

DON'T WASTE DOWN TIME WHINGING

This does not mean that you should sit by idly and lament poor levels of client flow. Rather, think if you can use the opportunity to attend to marketing and other administrative activities. As the old adage goes, 'if you can't hide it, make a virtue of it'. So use the time.

FINDING A BALANCE

Our time is one of our main assets. It needs to be carefully structured to meet the diverse needs and demands from clients and, of course, balanced against our personal and professional needs. We do not want to find ourselves tied down by our practice and constantly attending to clients in an unstructured and unboundaried way. To be available to clients at all and any times is not sustainable and arguably unboundaried. It also means the practice is running us and not that we are running our practice.

As someone said glumly to us 'One of my reasons for starting independent practice was to get away from someone running my work life, so I could get a better work–life balance. Now the practice is running my life in exactly the same way.'

Perhaps some of us need to recognize either that we are workaholics or that we have huge fears about our ability to sustain an independent practice. The practice does not in reality have a life of its own – we are its internal organs.

While there is obviously a need for a balance to be achieved, it is sometimes difficult to attain, especially in the early days of our practice while we gain confidence and a better understanding of client flow in our practice and our abilities.

If we were beginning again, a starting point in time management might have been the amount of time we wished to allocate to our independent practices in a given week. It might have been helpful to sit down, either with a year planner or with a spreadsheet open on our laptops. As in fact there were no laptops in those days, we might have taken sheets of paper and drawn a grid that listed the days of the week that we were available to see clients, as well as the time slots we wished to be available. There is nothing wrong with still doing it in this more old fashioned way. In fact for some of us, having a pencil in our hands and physically creating a plan may still suit us better. One of the reasons behind this book is a certain awareness that nobody told us these helpful things, so 'Don't do as I did, but make use of what I learned!'

HOW MUCH TIME SHOULD WE ALLOW PER CLIENT?

The answer to this question might be 'How long is a piece of string?' There is no set answer, sadly. The simplest thing is to consider the amount of time you wish to allocate to each client session and then to factor in time between client sessions. Sounds obvious, but we have often found ourselves forgetting this simple rule and overloading our diaries.

There is no legal or professional requirement for all your sessions to run for fifty minutes. It probably became the norm because early therapists found it useful to see people every hour, but realized they needed time in between clients. No great therapeutic reasoning there then, just pragmatism. However, it seems to have become a mystic 'rule' in many circles. Depending on need and who we are seeing, it may be more or less. As we have already said, unless you have rooms where you can accommodate clients who arrive early for their appointments in some sort of waiting area, you do not want there to be an overlap between clients. Not only will this disrupt you in your own sessions as you have to greet your next client while still finishing with another, but it may also prove disruptive to your personal life and intrude more into your home if that is where you see your clients.

Therapeutically, some therapists would also say that it is unhelpful for clients to be aware of each other, though in practice, when it has happened to us, it has not generally caused a problem. Where it has been an issue, it has been used in the therapy: for example, to raise issues of sibling rivalry.

Once we have allocated the amount of time that we have available during the week, we have found it is useful to divide up clusters of times into 'clinics' or practice sessions. The reason for this is that if you see clients on a back-to-back basis, there is a smoother flow than if they are spread unevenly throughout the day.

In the latter scenario, we are constantly moving in and out of professional mode and can find this tiring and disruptive. Of course we can also get it wrong and allocate too long a period for client work without a proper break, and this is not sensible for us or ethical for our client work.

MANAGING THE FLOW

As we go about organizing our clinical slots for the week, we have found that we need to ensure that we take sufficient breaks so as to replenish ourself both mentally and physically. When you choose to do this, and how often, is obviously a personal matter and will vary between therapists, but we find that taking a break of around thirty minutes to an hour after every third client seen seems to work. It also helps us to keep up-to-date client notes and records and ensure that correspondence and financial matters are attended to as the day goes along. Many of us suffer from procrastination and we are all susceptible to feeling overwhelmed with work, so we need to ensure that it does not get the better of us and dent our enjoyment of our practice.

Client flow is also important to manage. Large gaps in the day between clients, cancellations due to illness, a bus strike or traffic can prove disruptive and costly to us. Some readers may baulk at the idea of discussing with clients whether they can move their session to another time in the day to help with your client flow. However, if you feel that you have a good enough relationship with your client and that they would not feel pressured, you may be better off seeing if your 4 p.m. client can come at 2 p.m.

This allows you to fit in that couple who need an extra thirty minutes later and is better than either not having sufficient time between clients or leaving unfilled spaces in your diary. Spaces are unlikely to be filled unless you have an urgent referral. How you ask will obviously be important and your client should not feel under any pressure to change their appointment.

TRADITIONAL OR FLEXIBLE CONTRACTS AROUND SESSIONS?

Contacts with clients that require the client to 'sign up' for a year of therapy, perhaps several times a week, and in which the client undertakes to pay for all sessions, even if they are unable to attend, are increasingly rare. They reflect a particular approach to therapy that is unsustainable financially for most clients, especially in the current economic climate. Furthermore, at a practical level they are virtually unenforceable and give false (financial) security to the therapist.

The more flexible you are with regard to the terms of your practice, appointments and your time, the more accessible you will be to a larger number of clients. This is a win–win situation for you! It is important that you read this in the context of us being firm believers also in being ethical and professional. We are not advocating an 'anything goes' approach. It is absolutely right and proper for you to be able to charge for a session where you have not been given any, or sufficient, notice of a cancellation. What we think is untenable in sustaining a successful independent practice is for a therapist to charge for a session when the client has given a month's notice that they are going away on business or on holiday.

MAKING SURE YOU RECORD ALLOCATED TIMES

Once we have allocated time for client work during a given week, the next important step concerns how we record appointment slots. This may seem trivial or commonsense, but with the widespread use of PDAs and other handheld diary systems such as those found on mobile telephones, it may be more efficient and compelling to use these and similar devices for keeping your clinical diary. It is important, however, to ensure that you have backed up such information in the event of things going awry, such as misplacing your phone or, worse still, it being stolen.

Furthermore, it could have serious implications if personal information about your clients and identifying features such as their names were to fall into someone else's hands.

The age-old, tried and tested method of using a diary into which you handwrite appointments is, of course, acceptable, but perhaps limits your options if you undertake arranging your own client sessions. However, we have differing views on this. One of us still prefers a good old paper diary and a pen and finds it is frustrating to try to sit patiently while people trawl through their phones to find their schedules, and then backwards and forwards through the possible dates and times.

BEING AVAILABLE WHEN CLIENTS WANT TO SEE YOU

While you will need to decide when *you* are available to see clients, you also need to match this as closely as possible to the times when many of your clients wish to be seen. For example, if you work in or near a busy commercial centre, your clients may wish appointments before their work, during their lunch hour or after work. On the other hand, clients who are not working or work flexibly, as well as children and adolescents, may require sessions during the mornings and afternoons. It is sometimes a good idea to have a range of clinic times available to prospective clients so that you can meet several different needs until such time as a you develop a pattern, or a sense of when in the day most of your clients wish appointments. Whatever we decide, it is important that we try and avoid the trap of working all and any hours.

CLIENTS WITH PARTICULAR TIME NEEDS

Allocating time to special groups, such as children, couples, families and employees, may also need to be taken into consideration. This will be a reflection of the nature of the practice that you are seeking to develop. Couples, for example, will typically be available to be seen early in the morning, later on in the day or over weekends. You are less likely to find both partners free and available to see you during the middle of the day. The same may apply to families.

WEEKEND APPOINTMENTS

Weekend appointments are an interesting issue on their own. In today's society, people increasingly expect services of all kinds to be available to them at times that are not traditionally associated with independent practice. Weekends have become more popular among clients in recent years given the stresses that many of them experience during their weekdays and the difficulty some may have in taking time off from their work. Indeed, this may be a reflection of the very nature of the psychological or emotional problem that they present with: stress in managing their own time! Again, your flexibility in this regard may go a long way to helping to engage with such clients and also to develop your practice.

On the other hand, many therapists do not want their clinical work to intrude into their weekend time as this may correspond with time that they have set aside for their own personal lives. It may also not be possible to allocate such time, particularly if you see clients from home and you have your partner and children around at that time. Allocating time for clients is necessarily a task that requires you to achieve some balance between your personal needs and client flow. If you do not wish to work at weekends, you need to be very clear when potential clients approach you. If you choose to work one of the weekend days, perhaps consider a regular day off during the week, rather than work a six-day week. One of us has chosen never to see clients at the weekend, though will occasionally run training then.

HOLIDAYS

We need to take off times for holidays, and often want to try to match that to times of year when there are fewer clients around. It is sometimes difficult to predict client flow during a given year, until our practices have been running for several years. It is not entirely true, however, that all clients go on holiday during the August period and so client flow decreases at that time. Given that many other therapists may have decided to take off that time, ironically there may be increased demand on our services at that time.

School holidays may be a period of time in which to restructure our client sessions and decrease the number of client slots that we make available, even though we continue to practise at that time. The obvious times when client sessions may reduce are over the Christmas and Easter breaks, again often coinciding with school holidays. As mentioned, however, there is no longer a clear distinction and our decision to take leave at similar times may be based on our personal need rather than on client flow.

It is important to consider the length of time that we will be away and the frequency of our own absences from our practice. Clients who find that we are unavailable for lengthy periods of time may look elsewhere for help. Risk of damage to client flow possibly increases after two weeks' absence. Existing clients may drop out if we are away for too long – or indeed if they perceive that we have been. The e-mail below was received a month after a holiday period of two weeks. The client had been offered the opportunity to make an appointment for the week after the holiday, but had declined, saying she would be in contact after the break. In fact, she never returned.

> Hello Anne
>
> I hope you had a good holiday.
>
> Just thought I would be in touch now. Personally I think it has been difficult for me to book another appointment after you have been away for a while.

PRACTICAL ARRANGEMENTS FOR HOLIDAY PERIODS

Some people cannot wait until their problem can be dealt with and urgency may be a reflection of their distress. It is always worth leaving a message on your main contact number as to the length of time that you are away and when clients can contact you upon your return. It is also worth considering what other information you might put on in order to suggest that the premises are not empty, especially if this is your home. For example:

> The Counselling Service is closed until 26 June. You are welcome to leave a message but it will not be dealt with until after 27 June. Personal messages for Anne and Jonathan can still be left here.

This suggests that someone is still around to pick up personal messages. This may not be the case, but friends and family understand that.

In some cases, it may also be useful to give clients an e-mail address that they can use to contact you urgently if needed, so that the impact of your absence is minimized. Clients will appreciate your extra availability for emergencies, and most will not abuse this.

However, many therapists will have very clear views about this and will not want their holidays interrupted. Those practising in an entirely boundaried way will probably resist being available to clients, whether by phone or e-mail, while they are away or even between sessions. On the other hand, such willingness to deal with urgent issues may be something that helps to strengthen your relationship with some clients, even if it is the simple knowledge that they might be able to contact you should the need arise, which could prove containing.

Being away does not necessarily mean that your practice comes to a standstill. Many practitioners will develop either formal or informal links with a colleague who can stand in for them should the need arise, in which case it will be necessary to leave their contact details on your answering machine message, or pass on your colleague's details to a vulnerable client.

Remember that while you are away, you are not earning from your client work and so this needs to be taken into consideration when planning when and for how long you are absent. It is sometimes preferable to arrange your CPD and some supervision sessions at quieter times, if at all possible, so that the time allocated for these activities does not prevent you from earning professional fees at times when clients prefer to see you.

OTHER INTERRUPTIONS TO CLIENT WORK

There is more to managing time than simply allocating sessions or slots for clients. Not only will you wish and need to take breaks and holidays (and so will your clients), but there may also be interruptions to the flow of sessions due to a number of other situations or causes. These include your CPD training, your or a client's illness, moving home or moving premises, limits to a client's financial resources and an episode of counselling coming to its natural end before another starts.

In some cases, we can prepare for absences due to ill health. For example, if you have an elective operation and this has been scheduled some weeks or months ahead, you may be able to arrange your diary accordingly. The same applies to moving home or premises.

MANAGING TIME WITHIN CLIENTS' FINANCES

The matter of a client's financial limits is something that you may become aware of either at the outset of the course of therapy or during the course of it. This may have an impact on the length of therapy and therefore your available time slots. Some clients may tell you that they have limited financial resources for a course of therapy, in which case an ending may already be in sight from the outset. Others may become stressed by the financial implications of regularly attending for psychological counselling as this may have been unforeseen at the height of their distress when they began to work with you. Either way, this is a situation or context that will warrant open discussion with your client about their needs, your availability and what can be achieved in the available time.

ENDINGS

Psychological therapy usually comes to a natural end after an agreed number of sessions, or when the client's issue or difficulty has been resolved. In the latter case, therapists will agree to continue the course of therapy until the client believes their problem has been fully dispelled. This can be after many months, or indeed years, of therapy.

In the modern era, however, many clients may view therapy as a life-long relationship that is activated in episodes in which they have sessions at certain points through the course of their life, much akin to the relationship they might have with their own general practitioner. They may see their doctor from time to time with different medical problems, but with lengthy gaps between episodes of care. Or they may have a chronic condition necessitating more regular contact.

The same could be applied to psychological counselling in independent practice in which case a life-long relationship with the client could develop, although it is only activated when needed. Different approaches to therapy may need to be applied to different clients and problems. You may see some clients once and others for years. Flexibility in relation to how often you see your client will go a long way to developing a congruent, ethical and positive professional relationship with them. A happy client is bound to tell others how helpful you have been and this may go a long way to helping with your marketing.

TIME FOR ADMINISTRATION

Allocating clinical note keeping, letter writing, supervision and bookkeeping time is best done after you have allocated client time. Again, it is best to attend to these at quieter times, or when clients tend not to book appointments. It is logical to attend to administrative and related matters at times when clients are least likely to need appointments.

DEALING WITH OUT OF SESSION CONTACTS FROM CLIENTS

Perhaps one clear difference between working as an independent practitioner and working within a large multidisciplinary team such as the NHS is availability of the service. In the NHS, emergencies can be dealt with twenty-four hours a day, if not by a specialist counsellor or psychologist, then by staff working in an accident and emergency department of that service. The independent practitioner does not have such 'luxuries'. You will therefore need to consider whether you will leave your telephone on throughout the night or whether you will switch it off at a specified time so that clients cannot contact you directly during this time. Again, this will depend on the nature of the practice you are seeking to establish and some of the client problems that you have to deal with at a given time. You do need to think about the consequences of being too available, and reflect on your personal as well as professional reasons for being prepared to be available 24/7. Do you have a need to be needed?

It is normal custom in independent therapy practice to be flexible with clients in relation to their needs. After all, this is in part what clients are paying for: that is, the ability to access you more directly and if needs be more frequently. However, contact outside of arranged session times can become a form of extra therapy for free and it is important to address their needs with the client in face-to-face sessions and to discuss the use of out-of-session contact if this becomes necessary.

TIME SPENT ON FIRST APPOINTMENTS

Clients usually make their first contact with you by either phone or e-mail. It is important, however, not to let these methods of communication eat too much into your administrative time. You may also want to prevent therapy being conducted over the phone before you have properly contracted with the client and met them and assessed them in a face-to-face context.

For this reason, it may be best to use e-mail and texting only for setting up, changing and cancelling appointments, rather than for conducting extensive communications around how a client is coping unless of course you are an online therapist. In that case you will be trained in working with the different types of e-mails – therapeutic and contractual.

We recommend that you 'move' e-mail and text information to paid-for phone conversations or face-to-face meetings if it concerns therapeutic issues (i.e. not to do with your address or a change of the time of the session). E-mailing and texting can become time consuming and at some point, unless you work using text or the Internet as a medium for doing therapy, may adversely impact upon your time. We seem to live in a culture where it feels necessary to continue e-mail and text contact, when on the phone we would have ended the conversation. Don't be afraid to tell a client that their interests and needs may be best served if you could meet to discuss their issue if it requires more than a quick answer.

SPEND TIME ON YOUR RESOURCE BOOK

Working in independent practice does not mean that you work entirely on your own. Although you may not have the immediate support available to you as might be the case when working in a multidisciplinary team within an organization, you can have available to you a wide range of professional colleagues whom you can choose to work with. Every practitioner will reach the limits of their competence at some point. This can occur even a few times in a day! You will then need to involve other specialists or practitioners in the care of your client. In some cases, this may necessitate a referral to another specialist or it may proceed with a shared care arrangement. In such a case, you provide some aspect of psychotherapeutic counselling and more specialist problems, such as medical problems, are treated by a suitably qualified practitioner such as a psychiatrist. The most obvious contacts that should be developed and fostered are with the following professionals:

- Colleagues: other therapists or those with different availability or skills (e.g. child and family therapists, child psychotherapists, couples therapists and colleagues to provide cover when you are away).
- Psychiatrists.
- Health care.
- Other specialists (e.g. educational psychologists, physiotherapists).
- GPs who work independently.
- Advice agencies and help lines (e.g. Citizens Advice Bureaux, Childline, Samaritans).
- Your local hospital, community mental health team, A & E.
- Legal support for you and/or a client if needed.
- Your accountant.
- Your clinical supervisor.
- Your business mentor.

CONCLUSION

This chapter has highlighted one of the most important factors in providing an independent therapy practice: how you arrange your time. It has also started to address the need for you to develop a network of other colleagues and professionals who can support your practice even if you have only a loose professional relationship with them. This is picked up further in Chapter11. We have stressed the importance of flexibility in how you practise so as to make yourself available to as wide a range of clients as possible. The next chapter covers another important issue – managing your finances.

Below are some questions you might like to consider about managing your time when setting up your own practice.

Reflexive Points

- How much time do you have available to see clients?
- When in the day/week are you free to see them?
- How can clients make contact with you?
- Where can they leave messages for you?
- Do you offer e-mail/texting facilities for clients to contact you?
- How will you manage client flow and gaps in your diary?
- Who can you include in your list of professional colleagues?

Chapter 5

Financial Matters

INTRODUCTION

One of the most important aspects of running any business is to ensure that financial matters are well managed and controlled. Common sense suggests that we should plan ahead and prepare a budget in advance, before 'diving in' and potentially coming to regret some decisions. Of course, it is impossible to identify and anticipate every potential risk, but there are many that are common to counsellors and psychotherapists working in independent practice. We do not claim to be experts, and the experience and expertise of accountants and the business manager at your bank should not be overlooked. In this chapter, we consider a number of areas often regarded as the somewhat dry and boring areas of managing a practice, but they are core to its success. A private practice is more likely to fail due to neglect of practical issues than due to a lack of motivation or competence of the practitioner.

TRADING OR PRACTICE STYLE

A first decision is to consider whether you will be practising on your own or in some affiliation or partnership with other colleagues. This is not only a matter that has social implications in terms of whether we choose to work on our own or with fellow practitioners, but also has implications for where the financial, legal and clinical risk lies. For example, who is accountable for what happens in the practice and ultimately, from a legal perspective, who owns the service? We have chosen different routes: one of us has a company and the other is a sole trader.

There are four main practising or trading arrangements or styles that you can follow.

1. **Sole trader.** This is the self-employed individual who undertakes private, independent work, either as their sole means of livelihood, or alongside salaried employment. The defining features of this style are that you work on your own, are not accountable to other colleagues for financial matters pertaining to your service and carry all the risk associated with your own practice.

2. **An affiliate** is loosely connected with other colleagues. For example, you may have a website, cover for one another when a colleague is on leave or share practice rooms. However, you are not bound in any formal relationship. To this end, clients contract directly with the therapist concerned and not with an organization or company. Thus, while there may be shared organizational and financial interests, such as rooms, each of you is individually responsible for your own practice. You are still a sole trader but are loosely connected with others.

3. **A partnership** is an independent practice in which there is joint and shared responsibility for all aspects of clinical and organizational activity. Partners will normally have agreed a contract as to the nature of the practice as well as all matters relating to the finances. In a partnership, there will be a clear statement about responsibility for income and expenses, assets, objectives and strategies. There will also need to be clarity about what happens if the partnership is dissolved. For this reason, partnership agreements should always involve a lawyer to help to draw up a contract. It is rather akin to marriage in the civil world and therefore has important legal and administrative consequences. It may reflect some aspects of affiliation in that there will be formally defined roles between the different partners, but this is a more binding and accountable relationship.

4. **A limited company arrangement** may involve an individual trading either on their own or as a partner or affiliate. Its essence is that the practitioner works within a company that owns the assets and therefore income is paid to the company. This has implications for taxation, expenses and, of course, taking out money for an income. Tax is paid by both the company and the private individual who takes income from it.

These are important and potentially complex organizational, financial, clinical and legal arrangements that need to be thought through. As we indicated at the start of the chapter, we strongly advise that you seek suitable guidance from a specialist solicitor if you are in any doubt as to the kind of practice that you are seeking to establish. The essential questions to be established in advance are:

- Who owns the service or company?
- Who carries the risk?
- Who is legally responsible for the practice?
- Who is legally responsible for debts and unrecovered income?
- Who is legally responsible for clients' needs?

The answers to these questions will determine the kind of practice style set out above. This is also important in the event that you or your partner sadly dies while practising in any of the above configurations.

DEVELOPING A BUSINESS PLAN

The success of any business depends on a clear statement of objectives and intentions and a plan of how you will go about trying to achieve the aims of your practice. This can be more straightforward than first meets the eye. You need to generate a business plan, which serves as a template of your aims and intentions. Later it will be a benchmark by which to measure progress towards your stated goals.

It will also be an essential condition of a bank manager if you are seeking funding or financial support for your independent practice. Anyone providing funding wants to see:

- what you are trying to achieve;
- whether you have considered the potential caveats, pitfalls and competition that may thwart the success of your business;
- the extent to which you have considered the practical details such as fee structure and cash flow;
- if it conveys to you and to others a clear sense of purpose and awareness of the challenges and opportunities that you may face.

A business plan is considered a working document and should not be viewed as a static or inflexible set of rules for your business. Indeed, it is a document that should be updated and revised as your experience develops and new opportunities and challenges come to light.

However, there needs to be a starting point and the first draft of a business plan is just that. This document need not be too detailed or extensive as this may be constraining, but it should at least cover the salient aspects of what you intend to do and demonstrate awareness of the difficulties that you may come to encounter. It is similar to a research proposal in that it often follows a particular format and will normally set out your goals, objectives and strategy under five main subheadings. It is much like a road map. It is 'akin' to reality but only as a representation of it. It shows different features and routes may change at any time, and so may your destination, if you so choose. You can revise it at any time as new information or conditions come to light – it is only a template.

> **Belinda**: And you and Rob really did all this before starting out as independent practitioners?
>
> **Anne**: Well, actually I didn't! The most obvious reason is that when I began these things weren't suggested and there was no guidance to help me. The other reason was that I didn't have to borrow money so didn't have to convince the bank manager.
>
> **Belinda**: Would you do it differently now?
>
> **Anne**: I would definitely do much more on producing a business plan, so I had a clearer idea of where I was going – it all just kind of evolved for me, and I was lucky; no recession around then. As a sole trader, I might not need as detailed a plan as Rob has had to have in starting a company, but I would think it through much more.
>
> **Belinda**: So you are saying 'Don't do as I did, but do as I say'?
>
> **Anne**: Spot on!

The five subheadings mentioned above are as follows:

1. A statement of the overall goal and purpose of your practice.
2. Your objectives for developing the practice, how you will measure and monitor progress and success, and perhaps a statement as to why and how it fits in your professional life at this stage of your career.
3. The specific nature of the service that you are providing and the client group(s) that you are seeking to reach. This may include several sub-services (e.g. client work, teaching, supervision).
4. The market for your services as well as an honest account of the existing or potential competition.
5. Financial planning, which will include the professional fee that you will levy, how you will collect it etc. This will also include a profit and loss account and a list of all of your expenses, including those associated with setting up and managing your practice.

Belinda's comments were unrepeatable at this point, so we have included an example of an abridged business plan to show you the essentials.

Example of a Business Plan

Goal and purpose
The purpose is to develop an independent therapy practice to run alongside a salaried job as an IAPT counsellor in a GP practice, with a view to (a) establishing my presence in the independent therapy market locally, and (b) determining whether I can later expand this into a full-time practice.

Objectives
- To determine a need for a brief therapy service to cater for local clients.
- To establish limits with EAP services to take on local clients in need of such a service.
- To broaden my experience working with clients seeking therapy for anxiety and health-related concerns.
- To develop my supervisory skills and undertake occasional guest lecturing to counselling students.

Nature of the service
(a) Provide a therapy service to which clients can either self-refer or be referred by their doctor for a range of problems, including: depression, anxiety, worry, relationship difficulties, sexual problems, addictions, bereavement and loss and coping with health problems (I won't work with children until I have completed my child psychotherapy training).

(b) Offer a flexible approach to working with clients, starting out by offering a first assessment consultation and then negotiating further or ongoing therapy, depending on the nature and extent of the client's problem, and their motivation to continue in therapy. Clients will not be required to enter into a long-term contract. Flexibility will extend to providing both face-to-face and Internet-based therapy.

(c) Relating to the above, the service will be dynamic and will need to constantly monitor and evaluate progress in terms of progress in how the client's problem is treated.

(d) My practice will be supervised by an experienced clinical supervisor. I will complete my counsellor supervision course in two months and then be in a position to offer supervision to a trainee and qualified therapists. I will focus on supervising within a client-centred and brief therapy framework.

Market and competition
(a) I will approach local GPs, hospital specialists, lawyers and other therapists in the area and let them know about my service. I will offer to introduce myself to them in person and disclose my experience and practice. I will offer to give a short talk or presentation to them.

(b) Owing to the number of psychodynamic therapists in the area, my service can be differentiated from this given the more flexible and briefer approach to therapy. I will work in collaboration with these colleagues, referring longer-term clients to them, and receive referrals from them for CBT if needed.

(c) I will work collaboratively with other colleagues in the area, establishing links with therapists, health care providers and local training courses. I will publicize my presence and specialist interests by being available to local media for interviews.

Financial planning

(a) I will charge £75 for initial sessions and £50 for the follow-up sessions. I will draft a brief contact with my terms of business in order to make matters clear for patients. Fees will be payable at the end of a session to avoid risk of bad debt.

(b) I will work from home initially to reduce expenses. I will buy suitable chairs for my practice. Next year I will buy a new PC and software. I will use my existing phone. I will contact my insurers to put required insurances in place.

(c) I will print business cards and stationary for all practice correspondence. I will set up a dedicated e-mail address for professional correspondence. I will create a simple website with suitable search words to establish a web presence.

(d) I will consult an accountant to enquire about tax, pension and account planning management. I will retain an accountant on an ongoing basis in future years when turnover requires.

Belinda was still not totally convinced about whether she was going to bother with a business plan, as it felt too daunting at this point. She discusses this below.

> **Robert**: While it is important to have a business plan, it is also important not to feel too bogged down by it or constrained by having to include extensive detail.
>
> **Belinda**: I feel quite faint as I look at that plan. I'm overwhelmed.
>
> **Robert**: OK – let's not look at the whole thing, but go through it bit by bit. We'll take each of the five sections by themselves and spend some time thinking through what you want to put in them.
>
> **Belinda**: OK. That feels a bit more possible.
>
> **Robert**: Some practitioners spend excessive time aiming to produce the perfect business plan, but remember, just like that

⫸

road map, it won't reflect everything that we will encounter along the way. Go for a balance between your enthusiasm and energy for developing your business and attending to the practical details. If you allocate an inordinate amount of time to the business plan, that may prevent you from thinking creatively in areas that warrant your further attention.

Belinda: That sounds better – I need to take that on board before I can tackle the business plan! So let's have a go.

WHAT DO YOU NEED TO EARN?

It is essential to establish your personal budgetary needs. Assuming that your independent practice is not being set up for charitable purposes, you will need to consider and reflect on what sort of income is necessary for you to survive and potentially to thrive if you are to work in independent practice. If you are the sort of person who is used to a certain lifestyle but through your business plan you cannot see how an independent practice will support this, you may need to adjust either your financial expectations or your lifestyle if you are to avoid disappointment. In the end, if your income is going to be minimal, you are probably better off working in salaried employment, unless you have private means.

EXPENSES

Make a list of *capital* (one-off) and *recurring* (monthly or annual) expenses. Examples of capital expenses may include a laptop or personal computer, furniture and other business accoutrements. Luckily for therapists, we do not need expensive equipment, unlike dentists, doctors and some other professional practitioners who may have significant capital expenses. There are always recurring expenses, which range from keeping stocks of toilet paper to ensuring that the stationery cupboard is kept full and the mobile phone bill is paid.

PLAN YOUR BUDGET

This is best done on a monthly, quarterly and annual basis. The reason for this is that you can then not only keep a close eye on your monthly finances, but also develop an overview of trends over a period of time. In this way you will come to see when your busier times of the year occur and when it is likely to be quieter. You will also come to see when is the best time for you if you have spare cash to purchase new furniture if needed or upgrade your rooms if this becomes necessary.

Remember to factor in all of your sources of income to your private practice and not just your client work. For example, some practitioners working independently also undertake lecturing duties, do business consultancy and may have book royalties or examining fees that are due to them. These need to be included as part of your income.

HOW MUCH INCOME WILL I RETAIN?

As a rule of thumb, it is helpful to assume that approximately 50 per cent of what you earn in terms of your income will 'disappear' on taxation and other expenses. This will vary considerably from practitioner to practitioner, depending on such variables as whether you work from home, or rent, whether you need to travel, what CPD you undertake, whether you have administrative help etc. However, irrespective of the band of tax into which you fall, your expenses plus tax may consume up to half of your total income. This is sobering and may deter some from setting up in independent practice. Whoever said that independent practice is an 'easy option', 'cash cow' or 'money spinner' has obviously had no experience running a practice!

The fact that only half of income is retained can help you also to consider more carefully your fee structure and whether independent practice will pay. If, for example, you are charging £50 per hour, this fee level may seem less attractive when you come to find that your final take-home pay after deductions will be around £25 for that session.

Wherever you can, try to outsource at low cost any expenses that you may incur running your practice. It is ill advised to sign a long lease for expensive consulting rooms when you do not yet have a steady flow of clients. Equally, to employ a full-time secretary or receptionist at an early stage of your business may eat up all of your revenue and profit, and that is even before you have paid your taxes. Unlike large organizations that may budget for a loss for several years, professionals in practice should not countenance such risks.

USING OTHER PROFESSIONALS

It is advisable to meet with an accountant and/or a lawyer, who will be able to help you with budgeting, planning, claimable expenses, deductions and tax planning. This may seem an unwelcome expense at a time when there is still no income to count on. Nonetheless, a one-off consultation (which can later be claimed as a business expense) can save you considerable time and money later on, and potentially heartache too should your business fail. It is also an important step in your developing a professional network that includes not only colleagues to whom you can refer clients, but also other professionals who can support you in your quest to be successful in independent practice.

BILLING AND CHARGING

Setting your professional fee is one of the most vexing problems faced by the aspirant practitioner. It is one means by which we convey the relative value of our professional service. But many practitioners feel embarrassed discussing financial matters or handling money, which may seem an unwelcome intrusion into the 'pure' and sacrosanct therapeutic relationship. Nonetheless, reticence in this regard or being unclear of your fees and payment terms, and vague about communicating them to clients, inevitably leads to difficulties, stress and, sadly, litigation.

You must be clear about your fee from the outset with your client as this forms part of the contract. You cannot accept payment in a form other than money, such as bartering. For example, a client may offer his or her services as payment as part of the contract. The contract sets out an agreed fee and how you bill patients. Your fee and method of billing, and ultimately form of payment (e.g. cash, cheque, credit card), is determined in the relationship between you and your client and not by a third party such as a medical insurance company.

The only time this may differ is where the terms of the relationship are set out and underwritten by a third party such as a lawyer or via an EAP. Under these conditions, you are being contracted by the person who undertakes to pay your fee and therefore the relationship is a triangular one between you, your client and the third party paying for the treatment. Completing clinical paperwork may be a condition of EAPs paying you for your sessional work. It is therefore sensible that you discuss the contract and its terms with them before agreeing to work with the client, to avoid any unnecessary conflict of interest and subsequent refusal to pay for your work. It is always advisable to have the agreed terms put in writing to avoid any misunderstandings.

DETERMINING YOUR FEE

There are a number of issues you need to consider in establishing a fee:

- Will the first session be free, be half the normal session fee, cost the client more or be the same as subsequent follow-up sessions?
- Will you operate a sliding scale to make your service more affordable to a wider range of clients?
- Will there be a surcharge for extra skills and responsibility when working with children, couples or families?
- Will you offer a fee reduction to clients after a set number of sessions have passed (similarly to other areas of commerce, will the client benefit from 'bulk purchase' of sessions)?
- Will you review your fee annually or maintain it at an existing level for clients with whom you have already contracted?

You will need to consider each of these for yourself, although we offer some thoughts. Experience suggests that providing a first session free of charge to the client is potentially fraught with difficulties and can be self-defeating for the therapist. The first session, as we discuss elsewhere, is potentially the most important in therapy. To give this away free may send a confused message to the client. They may feel beholden to you for this act of 'generosity' or wonder how future therapy sessions will differ, and they might rethink the value of these. Such an incentive might work fine in a supermarket or in an optician offering a two-for-one promotion, but it may not work well in a professional, service-related activity.

A compromise position might be to offer the first session at half of your normal fee. This enables the client to decide if you are the right therapist for them at lower cost, but it also allows you to receive some payment for your time. If you choose this route, it is important that you are clear with the client that this is the reason why you are doing this.

The fee that you set will depend broadly on a number of different issues.

- Your qualifications, length of experience and reputation.
- Where you see clients and the cost to you of this, e.g. at home or on premises where you have to pay a rent, and your overall expenses.
- When you see them, e.g. do you offer less sociable hours and weekend consultations?

- The kind of work, e.g. do you see only individuals or do you also work with children, couples, families and undertake medico-legal work? Do you have specialisms? Do you work with a co-therapist, when working with couples? Does any of your work involve using the Internet, Internet-based voice communication such as Skype, or the telephone?

- What others local to you charge. You may or may not wish to differentiate yourself from others.

- The length of your session. There is no legal requirement for you to offer a fifty-minute session: some therapists may offer thirty minutes or even less when seeing children or people who are unwell. Others may offer significantly longer sessions – for example, when treating couples or for a first consultation – and therefore the charge must reflect this.

- The nature of the therapy that you provide, e.g. is it short- or longer-term therapy? Possibly for shorter-term therapy you may need to charge more as you have a higher client turnover and your sessions may require you to be more active.

- How clients pay for their sessions. There is greater cost to you if you are required to collect your fee after the client has left your consultation room. Sending out bills, reminders etc. adds to your costs. Clients who settle their bill in the session will demand less of your time and expense at a later point, although some therapists feel uneasy about handling money in sessions.

- The client's professional standing, e.g. you may wish to offer therapist colleagues or trainees a reduced rate.

REDUCED FEES

You may wish to offer a reduced fee to a client who is unable to pay your full fee. There is a difference between your full fee and a reduced fee, as opposed to a sliding scale. A sliding scale is a variable fee and is determined by each client's individual means, whereas a reduced fee is a predetermined fee that applies to all clients who qualify for this. A sliding scale is a challenging system to implement and manage as you require an honest account of the client's financial circumstances and any form of means testing necessitates a more extensive discussion with the client about their finances and personal situation.

Maria: What I've discovered is that when clients are paying for themselves, they want to work, and they want to work *now*. They don't want to stay for twelve weeks if they can do the work properly in less. They operate in a different world, and I think sometimes we've become sort of divorced from that world when we trained.

Sue: You see, that's where I have a lot of anxieties. I have a friend, and it took her a long time to get established in independent practice, who said that some clients will come and go, but usually she finds if they stay with her for three months, she knows they are ready to engage in the process of therapy.

Bob: It feels a bit much to have to wait three months and pay out, what, around £500, just to find out if you are ready to start therapy!

Sue: My anxiety is that I am taking money from my clients, and I'm thinking 'should I be working in a person-centred way?' where you know my belief is that it's a slow process. ... I'm struggling with that.

Bob: What would be wrong for me is if you slowed it down *because* you are taking money.

Sue: It's important for me to hear what you are saying because of course I wouldn't do that. I think my anxiety is that I am taking money and are they actually getting what they need?

Bob: So ask them.

Robin: I find with my own therapy, which I pay for, that sometimes I come out thinking 'that was a great session'. Other times I come out thinking 'Well, what happened there? Nothing. And I've paid for it.' I don't blame myself or my counsellor, because I'm a counsellor and know this happens, but do clients know this happens? Maybe I should say something. I would want my clients to tell me.

Bob: Otherwise, apart from anything else, if they go away dissatisfied, they're not going to recommend you to anyone else. Whereas if they are satisfied, they are your biggest source of other clients, almost regardless of what you charge. That sounds horribly commercially orientated, but I think ...

Robin: And we are in a business and need to make money.

Table 5.1   Setting your professional fee (this is a London practice example and regional variations may apply)

	Example		Advantages	Disadvantages
Decreasing scales	Session 1 Sessions 2–6 Session 7+	£100 £70 £50	• good for briefer therapies • 'loads' initial visits in which you are likely to work hardest	• may be too high for some clients • need a high turnover of clients
Variable scale	Medical insurers Company referrals EAPs Client self-funding	£100 £60 £40 £75	• have a more varied practice • more flexible	• same quality and amount of work for a different fee
Standard or low scale	All clients	£40	• good for long-term clients • good for trainees and when starting up • straightforward administration and billing	• need a large client base • difficult to charge higher fees later on, or to long-term clients
Sliding scale	Clients on income >£18k p.a. Clients below this pay according to means	£75 <£75	• fairer for a range of clients • broaden your client base	• you have to 'means test' your client • difficult to verify client's true income

COLLECTING THE FEE

Once you have established and agreed your fee, you then need to determine how you will collect it. Again, this forms part of the contract with the client. You will need to establish whether you will collect it at the end of the session or whether the client will be billed for it after the session has ended. If they are billed, you will then need to stipulate whether there is a time within which payment must be received. You, of course, then need to consider what you will do if the client has not paid within that time, as we discuss in Chapter 9.

You will need to decide whether you will accept cheque payments, cash payments, credit card payments or payments by a third party such as a lawyer or EAP. If the latter, as previously stated, you should have a written undertaking that the third party has (a) undertaken to reimburse you, and (b) will do so within a given period of time after being billed for these.

You may also need to consider the effect on your relationship with your client in terms of handling money in the session and also how you will deal with outstanding debts that are accrued in the course of therapy. (See also Chapter 7.)

Some clients experience financial hardship in the course of therapy. This may especially occur during a recession, when your client is made redundant, where the client separates or gets divorced, during periods of ill health or due to any number of normal but unforeseen circumstances. This should be openly discussed in the course of therapy. The options are to:

- reduce the fee during the course of financial hardship, with the understanding that the fee will revert to where it was before difficulties set in when things improve;
- allow the client to repay outstanding monies at a later point, accepting the inherent risk;
- terminate therapy and refer the client to other services, e.g. NHS or voluntary agencies;
- offer free therapy;
- maintain the current fee as agreed and allow the client to decide how he or she would like to proceed.

Which option you choose will depend on both your theoretical approach and your financial situation. What we have found helpful is that, as it arises, you consider the therapeutic consequences of each option in supervision.

MANAGING CASH FLOW

Every business requires a steady and predictable flow of income. This is firstly to ensure its survival, and secondly to underpin its future growth. Working in independent practice as a therapist is no exception. Although some therapists may be unfamiliar with how to handle aspects of their finances, just remember that you have handled your personal finance for many years. If your personal finances tend to be chaotic, you may need to pay particular attention to this area of the business.

Even though there are fewer overheads than for, say, a manufacturer, cash flow is still relevant for (a) your personal finances, and (b) the length of time that clients are in debt to you. Cash flow is vital to the future success of your practice and for your livelihood since you will derive income from your practice. Many of us work on the basis that clients pay us each session. If they do not, it is worth noting that clients take on average thirty days to pay an invoice when it is sent to them, so factor this in when calculating your cash flow. This length of time reflects normal commercial practice and so you will always be a minimum of one month behind in terms of invoice payments

On occasion, clients may pay you in cash. This is entirely acceptable, but do make sure that you provide a written receipt. There are two reasons for this. Firstly, there is no misunderstanding with your client that the session was paid for. Secondly, it is an important part of your record keeping for your Inland Revenue submission, and the documentation that your accountant will require.

Direct payment into a bank account by transfer is increasingly common and is efficient and safe. This has become more commonplace with Internet banking, and as fewer and fewer people use cheques. Providing details of your bank account on your invoice is helpful in this regard. Remind clients to put their name or some other way to identify them on the transfer so that you will know that it is that specific client who has paid.

Payment by credit or debit card is also acceptable if you have this facility. However, it can be expensive to set up and maintain a credit card facility. Banks not only charge a fee to provide the machine and service, but also take a small percentage (up to 5 per cent) of the fee collected. On the one hand, this method of payment is efficient and guaranteed. On the other, there is the cost that it will incur for you, as well as the discomfort some practitioners may feel handling the client's credit card. We know of very few independent practitioners who use this method currently.

BUSINESS BANK ACCOUNTS

Most of us dislike paying banking charges, whether on our personal account or for a business account, and we want to keep our costs to the minimum. A word of caution here. Some practitioners use their personal account to double as a business account. Your accountant is likely to advise you against this. It is best to keep separate records of your financial transactions, especially when it comes to your annual income tax submission. Furthermore, your bank will almost certainly frown on the dual use of a personal account, and may levy additional charges if it is being used as a business account.

There is also a further reason for keeping them separate. You are unlikely to benefit from the range of services available to small businesses if you do not have a business account. Loans, free banking and related services may not be available to personal account holders, whereas they are for those with a business account.

When choosing a bank for your business, do not be constrained by your longstanding loyalty to the bank that manages your personal account. You may find that other banks are more competitive and willing to offer you better rates. Many banks offer free business banking for the first two years of your business, which can prove attractive at this more vulnerable time in the development of your practice. It is worth comparing charges for the most common activities associated with business banking before opening an account. It is also helpful to choose a bank that has excellent online facilities so that you can manage your account in this way, or that has a branch nearby so that you can deposit cash and cheques with relative ease.

There are several ways in which to reduce your banking charges. Not all of them apply to all banks, since some charge for certain transactions that are free with other banks.

1. Pay by automatic direct debit or by standing order or by using Switch: these incur the lowest charges by banks.
2. Use cash received in your practice to top up your petty cash, rather than depositing it. (But do remember that it should still show up in your books!)
3. If your bank charges for cheque transactions:
   (a) draw cash from a service till using a debit card, rather than by cheque at a bank counter;
   (b) reduce the number of cheques that you write out;
   (c) reduce the number of times that you bank, as each time you deposit money a fee may be charged, so deposit several cheques in one go.
4. Use your credit card wisely. If you use the interest-free period, but pay it off each month, it is generally cheaper to use a credit card for small payments and expenses than to be overdrawn. Also consider a business credit card that gives you a bonus, such as air miles or supermarket points.
5. Set aside money for your annual income tax and related expenses by putting this money into a fixed deposit account that will at least earn you some interest, even in times of recession.
6. Do not keep large amounts of cash on your premises or in your home as this is obviously at risk of theft and also can increase your home insurance premium.
7. Avoid using your overdraft, as the interest charged on loans can prove costly over time.

DEBTS

Taking a service that you have agreed to pay for, and then not paying for it, is technically a breach of contract and can, in some circumstances, be deemed fraud. It is also damaging to your relationship with the client. Equally, it is important that we as practitioners avoid going into debt ourselves. This means good budgeting, good forecasting of our finances and not spending more than we earn. It is imperative, too, to set aside money for additional expenses, including taxes, National Insurance and professional indemnity insurances. Others are listed later on in this chapter.

PURSUING DEBTS

We have found the following points useful to remember:

1. Be clear about your contract and ensure your terms are agreed to from the outset.
2. Do not let debts linger: the longer the person is in debt, the smaller the chances you will have to recover it.
3. Pause or terminate therapy if an unpaid debt mounts beyond four sessions.
4. Never accept goods or services instead of payment. If the client is unable to pay, you may wish to make arrangements that they can pay off the debt over time in small instalments. However, no other means of settling the debt are acceptable.
5. Send a written reminder by recorded delivery every two weeks, restating your terms. This is essential if you are to pursue a claim against the client later.
6. Send a final warning at three months after the debt remains unpaid and state clearly your intentions. These may be to involve a professional debt collection agency or to take the matter to a Small Claims Court. (See also Chapter 9.)
7. If you decide to pass the debt to a professional debt recovery agency for collection, they will take a proportion of the fee that is collected. Many clients choose to settle their outstanding bill on receipt of a letter from a debt collection agency.
8. In exceptional cases, debts may need to be pursued in a court. This is unfortunate and potentially time consuming for the practitioner. The benefit must be weighed up against the cost that this could have in

terms of your time. For example, pursuing a claim for £250 in a court that requires your physical attendance could prevent you on that day from seeing three to five paying clients in that same time.

EXPENSES

Very obviously, your expenses for setting up and running the practice should not exceed the income generated. Inevitably there are expenses and these need to be considered before engaging in independent practice and certainly before signing up to any agreements that may prove costly to maintain. It is important to establish which expenses may be tax deductible, so it is always best to seek the advice and guidance of a chartered accountant. They will be able to provide up-to-date information about allowable expenses and their fees are also tax deductable.

The most common allowable expenses are as follows:

- **Rent:** seeing clients in independent practice needs premises unless you are providing therapy over the Internet. Regardless of whether you rent rooms, or you see clients from home, you will need to plan for this expense. A proportion of your expenses is allowable if you see clients from home: for example, wear and tear. Even if you work with clients over the Internet, you may be able to claim for the use of a study/consulting room at home. However, working at home can have financial implications when you come to sell your property and may incur capital gains tax.
- **Furnishing your rooms:** some therapists may wish to purchase furniture such as armchairs or a couch, filing cabinets, a computer or laptop, a desk etc. Typically, these are capital, one-off expenses. However, your accountant may advise claims to be spread over three years in terms of allowable expenses on your income tax return.
- **Utilities and cleaning:** electricity, heating, water, service charges, where these are fully attributable to your practice. A proportion can be claimed if seeing clients in your home.
- **Rates:** some practice rooms incur business rates from the local council and this expense needs to be factored in if you are renting rooms.
- **Telephone and mobile telephone usage:** a proportion may be attributable to your practice even if these are also your personal, private numbers. It is probably easier to have a separate mobile for business.
- **Professional expenses such as:**
  (a) clinical supervision, business mentorship fees and continuing professional development;

(b) journal subscriptions and academic books;
(c) membership of professional organisations and professional regis-
     trations (such as the BACP, BPS, UKCP, HPC);
(d) professional indemnity insurance and professional liability insur-
     ance;
(e) public liability insurance; this is essential if you see people in
     your home or in an independent practice not covered by this
     already.

- **Administrative and secretarial expenses,** including: typing, bookkeeping, printing, advertising and postage
- **Travel expenses:** you cannot claim for travel between your home and
  place of salaried employment but if you are required to visit a client
  at home or you run your practice as part of a business, then some
  travel expenses may be an allowable expense.

Do not forget that you will still be required to pay income tax on your
earnings, once your expenses have been deducted from your gross income.
Ensure that you keep some of your income aside for this. Your accountant
will be able to advise you in this regard and give you an estimate of what
to expect to pay.

Ellie: I realize that I don't know all that I could claim for. Is it
really worth me paying out for an accountant? Or will I in fact be
paying them more than they save me?

Carole: I don't think so. Mine does all the bits I haven't a clue
how to do, like percentage of my car expenses, and of my telephone bills. I am sure I save more that I pay out, and it's kind of
comforting as well to know that it's all legal and above board.

David: What I'm not good at is remembering that twice a year I
will need to pay out for income tax! So it's a bit of a scramble
round then.

Ellie: Twice a year?

David: Yes after year one, I paid out what was owing from the
previous year and then later half of what might be due in that tax
year, based on last year.

Ellie: That sounds complicated!

Carole: That's why it's worth having professional advice!
Though in fairness, I do have several colleagues who do their
own accounts and tax forms every year.

REDUCING YOUR EXPENSES

There are numerous ways to reduce your capital and recurring expenses. Some of these we have already mentioned, but to sum up:

1. See people from your home, rather than sign lease agreements for the use of premises, until you have a steady flow of clients.
2. Rent premises by the hour if possible and try to see clients 'back to back' to save unnecessary extra travel and disruption.
3. Cluster your clients into 'clinics'. If you are constantly travelling to and from your practice rooms, or spread your clients throughout the day, this will prove disruptive and ultimately more costly to you.
4. Have your clients pay at the end of each session so that you do not incur further expenses in collecting the fee later on.
5. Use e-mail for communication of 'letters', contracts and billing.
6. Arrange group supervision rather than one-to-one supervision.
7. Advertise only where there is likely to be real, direct and measurable gain.
8. Use bottles of water or a water jug and glass rather than a water cooler.
9. Accept cheques and cash as payment rather than credit cards.
10. Avoid borrowing money for any aspect of practice as this is likely to incur interest and related charges.
11. Share facilities and resources with others wherever you can, such as a waiting room, a secretary etc.
12. Engage a 'virtual' secretary; somebody whom you can communicate with via e-mail and digital recorders, who can do your billing for you, prepare letters and reports etc., so that you do not carry the overhead cost of employment.
13. Find a good accountant.

CONCLUSION

This chapter has described some of the important financial and business related aspects of developing your practice. These underpin all successful practices and so they require careful attention. One of the attractions of running your own practice is that you can develop and have your business skills alongside your clinical ones. Regular reviews of all aspects of your business, including client billing, practice expenses, tax planning and banking among others, is necessary. A practice mentor, accountant and bank manager can all advise and guide you to help streamline your practice and help ensure its success. The questions below may help you to consolidate the thoughts from this chapter.

Reflexive Points

- Do you have access to specialist financial and business support?
- Have you considered opening a dedicated business account for your practice?
- Have you provided for your tax bills?
- Do you have a pension? Have you discussed this with a financial advisor?
- Do you have a system for invoicing clients?
- Do you have a template letter setting out your terms of business for clients?

Chapter 6

Practical Aspects of Client Work

INTRODUCTION

In Chapter 7 we consider the therapeutic issues of working with clients in an independent setting, and in Chapter 5 fee scales were explored. Here we look at other practical aspects of client work. There are no 'correct' ways of doing things, and very rarely any absolutes. Issues are raised and some suggestions made, but it is up to you to tailor your client work in the way that seems most appropriate and ethical to you. You may already be an experienced independent practitioner, and so this will be old ground for you. It could still be worth reading on, as we have found that writing about this has made us rethink and update some of our own practices.

The first contact has been made, often by telephone, and an initial appointment has been agreed. The hour has come for the first appointment. You have had numerous first appointments before, but this is the first one as an independent practitioner. What is different? The most obvious thing is that the client has probably chosen to work with you, rather than being allocated by an organization or through a referrer. There are some instances when this may not be true: for example, if you are accepting a client through an EAP or a fellow professional. However, in most instances, the client is coming because he or she wishes to engage with you.

PRE FIRST SESSION INFORMATION

Going back a step, how easy have you made it for a client to find you without any problems? When you make an appointment, it is helpful to offer to send a map or written directions. A letter or e-mail with these directions is also a good way of confirming in writing the information about the date and time of appointment, particularly if the initial contact has been by telephone.

It is not a bad idea to get a friend to try out your directions before you start using them with clients. You know that 'second road on the left' ignores that tiny passageway that does not take traffic, but will the client? Many clients coming by car will use a GPS system to find you these days. Do suggest they check that it is accurately pinpointing your address. Routinely putting in the postcode for one of us actually landed people in a neighbouring village!

If clients are likely to come by public transport, give bus numbers, or a nearby rail station. If possible, say how long an average walker will take from the bus stop or station, and any useful landmarks to find your building.

If you have a waiting area, include this in your directions, and whether they just sit down there to wait until you appear, or have to ring a bell to let you know they are there. If you do not have a waiting area, and are likely to have had a previous client with only a short gap between, think of what you might need to tell a new client. Do you expect them to wait outside or in their car until the appointed time? If they are on foot, is there somewhere they can wait nearby (a coffee bar, perhaps) if they are very early or it is raining?

Example of a Pre-session E-mail

Dear Sam,

It was good to talk with you today. I am attaching a map and directions, as promised, and look forward to seeing you next Thursday 20 May at 10.30 a.m.

There is plenty of parking, on either the drive or the gravelled area. If you arrive very early, you might like to know that the village shop has a small coffee area. I do not have a waiting room, and may have a client in the appointment slot before yours, so it would be helpful if you could wait until 10.30 before ringing the bell. I hope that is OK with you.

Warm wishes
Anne

As you read this, you may have thought that this is treating the client like a child, but bear in mind how nervous many clients are as they come to the first appointment. If they have problems finding you, it can only be your fault as there is no institution or organization behind you. (Of course, some clients will blame themselves as that is part of their script.)

CONTRACTS AND CLIENT INFORMATION

Sam, our mythical client, has arrived safely and at the appointed time. It is possible that you have sent him some information about counselling and about how you work before the appointment, or that he has looked at your website. However, it is wise not to assume anything, even if your client says that he has read the leaflet you sent him. The content of contracts and issues of informed consent are discussed elsewhere, but at a practical level, it is important to be sure that Sam understands what the wording actually means. So you could either ask him if he wants to clarify anything, or even briefly run through the main points again.

This can be done without implying that he cannot understand the contract by using a sentence such as 'If it's OK with you, I'd just like to check that I've covered all the practical aspects of working together, by running through the main points again.' Alternatively, you could go through the content with Sam, and then give him the written version. In independent practice, it is a good idea to have a written contract, since it is you and not an organization's system who will have to sort out any disputes about cancellations, payments etc.

At this point, you may want Sam to fill in an intake form. If you have a waiting area, you could ask Sam to arrive fifteen minutes early for the first session, telling him that it will be in an envelope with his name on, ready for him to complete. This saves time, though some practitioners may prefer to ask Sam the questions themselves and jot down the answers. There is often additional information that comes out by doing it that way, either through what Sam says or through body language.

Depending on the length of your contract and intake form, as well as the questions Sam may want to ask you, this may have taken a large part of the session. Sam may be beginning to wonder if you are ever going to get to the point of what he has come for – his issues. It can be tempting to skip over these aspects of beginning your work together, so that you can begin the therapeutic work.

There are various ways of overcoming that temptation. The first possibility is to make it clear in the initial contact that the first session will be solely or partly about setting up the way you will work together. At least then, Sam is prepared. You could suggest a shorter session (e.g. thirty minutes) to do this. If you were working in an organization, much of this work might have been done by an intake assessor rather than you. However, you are now on your own.

Another possibility is that you convey beforehand that in this initial session, both of you will be deciding whether or not you can work together, so you will not be delving very deeply into Sam's issues. For practitioners who have a strong emphasis on client autonomy in their approach, this also communicates to Sam that he too has choices – he doesn't have to work with you simply because he has made a first appointment.

You could decide that first sessions will be longer than a 'normal' session. So you might want them to be an hour and a quarter or and hour an a half, rather than fifty minutes or an hour. If you adopt this solution, you will need to be very clear with Sam that it is for the first session only. It is a break from the boundaries and for some clients and practitioners might set the scene for further ruptures.

There are also fee implications involved in the first session. If it is not a mainly therapeutic session, are you comfortable with charging Sam your full fee? There is nothing wrong with doing so, as it is your professional time and you know that what you do in this initial time together will influence the therapeutic relationship. However, some independent practitioners prefer to offer the initial session at half their normal fee, or even as a free session, as discussed in Chapter 5.

Although neither the contents of a contract nor the fee structures are the focus here, it is worth mentioning one point that has legal and financial implications. It should include a statement about fees. Cristofoli (2002) maintains that if a practitioner does not have a written agreement with a client regarding fees, 'there is scope for the latter to argue about what has actually been agreed to be paid'. There is perhaps also an implication here that both client and practitioner should sign and date the contract; otherwise, the client could claim that he or she had not expressly agreed to it. This is another practical task for the first session.

Anne: So, Sam, can I just make sure I've remembered to tell you everything for this session. It lasts for fifty minutes and the fee is £25. If we decide to work together, all sessions are that length, but the fee is £50. The reduction today is because it gives you a chance to meet me and decide if you think I can help you. Is that OK with you?

⇒

> **Sam**: Yes that's fine, and you've already sent me a contract which I'll sign and bring back if we are going to arrange another session. Have I got that right?
>
> **Anne**: Yes, that's right. So today I'll be asking quite a lot of questions, more than I will normally if we work together, so I can check that I may be able to help you.

At this point in reading this chapter, you may be feeling frustrated. You started up your practice to work therapeutically with clients, not to get involved in all these boring details. However, McMahon et al. (2005), in exploring the contracting and information-giving aspects of a first session, state that 'the boundaries and security it offers the client, as well as the sense of professionalism it projects, far outweigh these concerns'.

FOCUSING AND GOALS

Many clients arrive with hazy ideas of what they expect from working with you, or how long the process might take. When in paid employment, these aspects may well be a matter of the organization's policies, and the practitioner will simply state how many sessions are available to the client – that this is a one-off consultation, six sessions are available or open-ended work is a possibility.

The independent practitioner has a more complex task. There is a greater need for clarity about the client's expectations. If they can afford and wish to engage in open-ended work, that needs to be ascertained at the first session. Of course, clients may, and do, change their minds during the process, but it is not ethical practice to assume that clients will be able to stay for as long as it takes. They may have mentally set aside a certain sum that they can afford to spend, or a certain amount of time, though feel reticent to tell you this for fear of giving offence. Therefore, it is up to the practitioner to raise the subject in order for both parties to have realistic expectations of what might be achieved.

Simple questions such as 'When we finish working together, how will you know if it has been worth while? What will be different, Sam?' both signify that there will be an end and focus Sam on what he hopes to achieve. If such questions are followed up with 'Do you have any sense of how long it will take us to get to that place?' it may help him to express the length of contract he is visualizing.

Of course, it is quite possible that you may get the answer 'I don't know' or 'I thought you'd tell me that.' In that case, it can be useful to ask 'And if "Don't Know" had a voice, what would it be saying?' However a bizarre question that may sound, it may jolt Sam into saying what he in fact does know at some level, but has chosen not to reveal. You might prefer a different version: 'What would you like me to have said, if I had told you?'

Thinking about the focus or goals helps the client to allay fears that they might get trapped into working with you 'forever', which can be a very genuine concern when meeting an independent practitioner. One of the myths about being self-employed is that we have a desire to keep our clients longer than they need or wish to stay, as it brings in income. However, as Tyler (2003) asserts, 'Discussing money issues with your clients, potential or existing, can be challenging for both parties.' Perhaps that is why we sometimes shy away from it.

It also helps you to plan this work, and to know when you might have a client space free again, thus enabling you to respond to enquiries from other potential clients about likely availability. There are obviously also therapeutic reasons for focusing on outcomes, but these are not under discussion here.

A slightly different issue might be if your practice involves working with clients referred to you by a company or a GP, for example. There you may have an allocated number of sessions that the provider will pay for. Many of such contracts explicitly state that you may not enter into a private arrangement after these contracted sessions have terminated, or will state that there must be a gap of at least three months. If so, when asking the client about their expectations, you do need to be clear about that, and agree what may be possible to work on in the time you have. If you do not know what they have been hoping to achieve, it may lead to a disgruntled or disappointed client at the end of your work. Apart from the lack of professionalism on your part, pragmatically it does not make good business sense to have a disgruntled client. Potentially, they are one of your best sources of future clients, as reputation and word of mouth recommendation are key factors for a successful business.

Of course, work must never revolve round your clients liking you, and some clients may still end up disappointed whatever you do. Cristofoli (2002) recommends that the contract should include the words ' the Therapist gives no guarantee that the therapy and provision of services will result in an improvement to the Client's mental or physical condition or general well being'.

REVIEWING AND EVALUATING WITH CLIENTS

Whether they are employed or self-employed, practitioners have differing views on both the necessity for reviewing their work with clients and how this is best carried out. If you want to develop a successful business, it is an essential part of your work; otherwise, you may be making unfounded assumptions about what is going well and what is not, and attaching spurious reasons for both.

There are two aspects to reviewing your work – the therapeutic work with clients and the overall evaluation of your practice – and many ways of doing this. One obvious element is 'do clients return, and do they recommend you to others?' While accepting that clients can end their work with you for all manner of reasons that have nothing to do with the quality of the therapy itself, if you are getting a number of non-attenders, cancellations, one-off sessions or potential clients not turning into actual clients after a first contact, something may be going wrong.

If you are in supervision, then this is obviously one place where you can discuss how to evaluate your work, and what to do about your findings. So finding a supervisor who also runs a successful independent practice is a good move. There could be a temptation to stay with a supervisor who has supervised your employed work, even if she solely works in an employed capacity, since she knows you and your therapeutic work well. While such arrangements can work well, it is worth checking whether she has any knowledge of the complexities of running an independent practice. If your discipline does not require you to be in supervision, or you want to stay with the same supervisor who does not have the necessary experience, then finding a mentor or a 'critical friend' could be an advantage. Choose someone who is able to give you developmental feedback in a helpful manner, and has the necessary expertise, not someone who will simply tell you what they think you want to hear.

A useful ongoing means of knowing how the work is going with clients is to end sessions with a mini review. You could ask questions such as:

- What have we done that's been helpful today, Sam?
- Are there any particular parts of the session that you want to take away and remember?
- Is there anything that hasn't been helpful?

If clients are routinely in the practice of evaluating sessions, not only do they engage therapeutically, but when it comes to an end of contract review, they are in a much better place to gather their thoughts, and make a full and helpful response.

While these mini reviews are probably best carried out in a conversation, final reviews or evaluations are usually more use to you if they are written. It might be helpful to flag up at the first session that you ask clients to fill in an evaluation form when they finish their work with you. Some people even give a copy of it at that point, so that clients have lodged the questions somewhere in their minds. If you do this, also expect that the client may have misplaced it by the final session, so have another copy ready.

There are various ways of administering an evaluation questionnaire. You might choose to give it to the client on the penultimate session, and ask them to fill it in at home, bringing it back to the last session. You could ask them to fill it in during the session, or you could give it to them to take away at the end of therapy and send it back to you. The risk with the last way is that it may never come back, while the advantage is that some clients will be more honest if it is after the work has ended. Giving a stamped addressed envelope, although an extra cost to you, brings a higher rate of returns.

Often when people are employed, feedback and evaluation tends to centre on the relationship and process. When running your own business, you will want to ask about other things too. So some of the areas you address in your questionnaire are shown in the list below. Here we have put the practical questions first, as that follows the chronological order of the process. There is also an argument for putting them last, so you get the therapeutic information as fully as possible.

- Where did you find my name?
- How helpful did you find our first contact?
- Were the details I sent you useful?
- What else might have been useful to know before we met?
- Were the environment and the counselling room satisfactory?
- Was the first session useful?
- What did I do that was helpful to you?
- What could I have done that would have been more helpful to you?
- What has changed for you during our work together?
- Any other points you would like to comment on.

Some of these questions only require a yes or no answer and you want more than that. Therefore, when you design your evaluation form, you could ask the client to comment on the questions. You might also consider using a scaling system for the client to circle a number. This is particularly valuable if you use scaling in your therapeutic work. If you do that, avoid using an odd number of digits, as if in doubt people often circle the midpoint number. With an even number, this cannot happen. If they have to score marginally above or below the middle, at least this gives you a little more information. So, for example,

0　　1　　2　　3　　4　　5　　6　　7　　8　　9　　10

allows the client to circle 5 (the midpoint), while

1　　2　　3　　4　　5　　6　　7　　8　　9　　10

means that they have to choose either 5 or 6, 5 being less than halfway and 6 being above halfway.

It is worth emphasizing to the client that you value and take note of feedback, even though they cannot ever know whether this is true or not. If you have a couple of sentences to that effect on your questionnaire, though, they may be encouraged to take time to fill it in thoughtfully. Obviously, the client should be thanked for doing this.

You could consider using a system such as the CORE model for evaluation, particularly if you have been used to using a particular one when employed and found it helpful. Check that it covers all the areas you wish to evaluate and be aware of the costs involved. However, 'it might be beyond the needs and purposes of a private practitioner, given the time and effort such a model would take' (McMahon et al., 2005).

CLIENT RECORDS

It could be that one of the reasons you have chosen to go into independent practice is that you want to get away from 'all that record keeping'. In our view, there is an even greater need to be scrupulous and meticulous in keeping records of client work when in private practice. At a basic level, if things go wrong, it is down to you, without the backup of an organization. While, at present, there is no legal requirement for therapists (Bond & Mitchels, 2008) to maintain any client record, most professional associations would require justification for members *not* doing so. Independent practitioners who fail to do so are potentially putting themselves, their business and their clients at risk.

Basic information

All information that you keep about clients must be physically protected against such things as fire, flood or theft, and also be kept in a manner that ensures their confidentiality against being read or used by anyone else. If you arrange the former, you are probably also safeguarding the second criterion.

You need to have information about the client so that you can contact them if an appointment has to be changed, or if your car breaks down on the way to your practice premises. It is no longer possible to phone your agency or workplace and ask them to do this for you. So you may have to have one set of records at home, one in your consulting room if you do not work from home and possibly even a coded entry in your diary or your mobile phone.

This set of information should be kept separately from your therapeutic notes, and involve some system that allows you, but not a burglar, to match up the two. It may be highly unlikely that a burglar would have the slightest interest in your work, but records could be stolen as part of a break-in, simply because they are in a filing cabinet and might be thought to contain useful financial information. If they are not looked at until the burglar has got safely away, and then found to be of no value, they might be discarded, only to turn up in someone's dustbin or on their front lawn.

As Symes (1994) says, clients have a right to expect practitioners to guard their confidentiality. Basic information should contain name, address, contact telephone numbers, e-mail address etc., and possibly an emergency contact person.

Therapeutic notes

If you have found a useful form for making notes when on placement or in employment, then use that as a template for developing your own. Otherwise, you have to decide what you choose to write.

Bond and Mitchels (2008) give useful pointers to record keeping. These include that it should:

- be adequate, relevant and not excessive;
- be accurate and, where necessary, up to date;
- not be kept for longer than necessary;
- respect clients' rights;
- be stored securely;
- have technical security (IT systems).

What is adequate but not excessive? A good starting point might be to keep your records factual, containing only what the client has said or explored. 'The client said . . .' or 'Themes explored were ...' are useful phrases. You need to remember that under certain circumstances the client or a court may ask to read you notes, so it is probably best to avoid musings or hypotheses in your records.

In a busy independent practice, it is easy to 'forget' to write up client notes soon after a session. Nevertheless, if you have seen a number of clients in a week, your records may not be accurate when you sit down to have an evening of catching up on a Friday night. This is a lesson learned from bitter experience!

It is difficult to know how long to keep client records, as you may run out of storage space in a filing cabinet over the years. It is wise to keep them for at least as long as any complaint can be brought against you through your professional association. It may be necessary, therefore, to have one place for current clients, or immediate past clients, and one for those you ceased working with over a year ago, for example.

Finally, there is an issue of who owns the records. In independent practice, they belong to the therapist unless you and the client agree otherwise. Very occasionally, a client may ask you for a copy of your notes. If this is the case, before you pass them over, you should clarify whether you retain ownership, or whether the client 'holds both ownership and possession' (Bond & Mitchels, 2008). It would be wise to have whichever agreement you make in writing and signed by both of you, to avoid a later dispute. This leads us into the matter of data protection and access to information.

Data protection

The Data Protection Act 1998, which came into effect in 2000, requires that you should inform the Information Commissioner's Office of personal data being held on computer (automated files). There is an annual registration fee (currently £35). Its purpose is to open up greater transparency and ease of access by any citizen to information held on them. The Freedom of Information Act (2000) applies to public bodies, and in the vast majority of cases will not apply to the independent practitioner.

You may be thinking at this point that, thankfully, this does not apply to you as you solely keep handwritten records. However, before skipping to the last part of this chapter, read on to check that it really does not apply. As Jenkins (2002) states, it is a cultural change and is a 'particular challenge to counsellors and psychotherapists as a professional group, because of the very centrality of recording within their established practice'.

Do you keep any information at all about clients on your computer? Have you sent an e-mail, or received one, from a client about changing an appointment, or some other matter? Do you word process your notes? Perhaps the EAPs you work for send information by e-mail and require you to complete forms online. This would be construed as personal information related to an identifiable living person, and as such it would fall under the terms of the Act. If you ever consider undertaking any therapeutic work online, you certainly should register.

You do need your client's permission to store any information on your computer, and clients have a right to ask to see such information. One of the principles of the Data Protection Act is to give a client the right to access information being held about them – 'subject access right'. They have to apply in writing, pay a fee and possibly prove their identity. This allows them to see structured manual files (paper held) and computerized records.

Handwritten notes may or may not fall under the terms of the Data Protection Act. If they are part of a specific health record, part of which is kept on a computer, then it would apply. However, even if they are not part of such a record, there are still some circumstances under which access might be permitted. It depends on whether it is classed as a 'relevant filing system', i.e. one that could be accessed easily. So your small box file with cards with solely a record of dates attended and contact details, easily accessed by someone not familiar with the contacts, is a relevant filing system, and would not come under the Act. Structured manual files, properly organized, cross-referenced, maintained and securely stored, would.

Bizarrely, as Bond and Mitchels (2008) point out, a practitioner who keeps haphazard records has much less chance of their client being able to access their records than one who maintains a proper filing system or computerized records. However, that is not to be read as an invitation to sloppy record keeping!

Jenkins (2002) offers a useful statement from the Office of the Data Protection Registrar about paper-held records:

> If you have only got information which falls within a 'relevant filing system', i.e. non-automated files, or you've only got a relevant filing system and non-automated accessible records, i.e. paper-held records, you do not need to register, where this is the only data you have. If you also have automated records, you do have to register under the Act.

You need your client's permission to store any information on your computer, and clients have a right to ask to see such information. It is a complex area for the independent practitioner and there are useful sections in both Bond and Mitchels (2008) and Jenkins (2002) about the Data Protection Act. The Office of the Data Protection Registrar is also usually extremely helpful and patient when dealing with practitioners' enquiries about the need to register or not. There is also a checklist on www.dataprotection.gov.uk to help you make your decision.

Incapacity and therapeutic wills

Sadly, there are times when an independent practitioner dies suddenly, or is incapacitated in a way that means that they cannot deal with the practical aspects of contacting clients. There is a need to think this through at the start of your practice so that your clients are not left 'unheld' therapeutically, or your family or friends are left trying to sort things out at what may be a traumatic time for them.

If you have a supervisor or a mentor, they may be willing to act for you. You could choose a fellow practitioner. Once you have agreed this in principle, put it in writing and make sure that your next of kin or someone likely to be dealing with your affairs knows how to contact this person. The named person will need an up-to-date list of your clients, plus anyone else who may need to know the circumstances, such as referrers and your professional contacts. This is where many of us fall down. We make the agreement, and for the first few months are meticulous in updating our list and putting it with the instructions about how to contact the person who will take over the information giving. Then we put it on our 'to do' list but never quite get round to keeping it up to date. Try to make it a regular task, in the same way that you keep your accounts up to date.

> At the time of writing, there was a good example of how this can pay off. One of our supervisees had been in a workshop we were running when this topic came up. Afterwards, we had a conversation where it transpired that we had never discussed it in supervision – which just shows how even when we are experienced, we can forget the basics! So the supervisee sent a list of all her clients with contact details, and went off on holiday, only to be stranded by the Icelandic volcanic ash cloud, without having client details with her. Thank goodness we had put this into place before she went, as clients were able to be contacted and appointments cancelled.

Part of the agreement should be about the limits of the named person's involvement:

- Will they simply be responsible for giving the information?
- If necessary, will they arrange to see clients for a one-off session?
- Will they arrange other counsellors to work with a client's sense of loss or abandonment, if that is appropriate?
- If a death is involved, are they at liberty to give information about the funeral arrangements?
- If it is a serious illness, what information should a client be given?

Some practitioners, engaged in long-term work, may choose to tell their clients that such a process is in place. There is a time cost involved for the person responsible for this task. Clarify how they will be paid for the hours they put into doing it. It can take much longer than anticipated, and it is also draining. There are no right answers to these questions, though you do need to have thought them through.

CONCLUSION

Much of what has been written about in this chapter might well come under the heading of 'practical boundaries'. Since there are no organizational constraints, it can be easy for independent practitioners to ignore these, or become slack in maintaining them. If this happens, it is quite likely to impinge unconsciously on the therapeutic boundaries. If, however, you attend to the practical side of client work, you are organizing your practice within an ethical and profession framework, and can concentrate on the therapeutic process when with your clients, which is most probably why you wanted to do this work in the first place.

Reflexive Points

You might like to work through some of the list below, in order to think through how you will deal with the issues raised in this chapter.

- What pre-session information do you think would be useful for clients? Do you need to organize any part of that now?
- Does your contract need reviewing, and do you routinely have all the client information you need?
- How have you decided to review and evaluate your practice? If you are already doing this, is it giving you the information you need to maintain a successful business?
- Think about both the content and security aspects of your record keeping. Are you satisfied that if a client asked you about these, you would be able to give them answers that they would find reassuring?
- Have you made arrangements for unexpected incapacity or death? If so, do you need to review them to make sure they are still appropriate? If not, begin to decide how you will tackle this issue.

Chapter 7

Engaging with the Process

INTRODUCTION

As every therapist is aware, engaging with a new client is potentially the most significant moment in psychological therapy. The reason for this is that it not only affords the therapist important information about the client, the problem, motivation and needs, but also helps to clarify what may lie ahead and raises potential difficulties that may affect the future of the therapeutic relationship.

There may be overt or latent problems in engaging with clients. These need to be addressed if therapy in any context, especially independent practice, is to proceed without unforeseen difficulties. The process of engagement may be more challenging than when working within an organization, such as in a GP practice or in an NHS hospital, because in independent practice there may be fewer established structures and referral pathways or administrative backup that facilitate referrals within organizations.

In order to illustrate the points being made, we have interspersed the text with extracts from an actual telephone transcript between a prospective client and a therapist working in independent practice. We hope this conveys how a relatively brief conversation can help to reveal aspects of the client's problem, motivation and compatibility for therapy, as well as whether the client will accept the terms of the therapeutic contracts, such as your fee, payment and cancellation policy.

Working in independent practice requires you to begin to make an assessment of the client and his or her problem right at the point of first contact. This is important because it is at this stage that you need rapidly to decide whether you can work with the client. There may be problems with the client's pattern of attendance for sessions, payment for sessions and expectations of therapy, and some of these may first become evident in the very first therapy meeting.

Jay Haley, an eminent therapist, said that 'If therapy is to end properly it must begin properly – by negotiating a solvable problem and discovering the social situation that makes the problem necessary' (Haley, 1976). The therapist in independent practice needs to take active responsibility for engaging with the client, assessing his or her problem and determining the next stages of therapy, if there is an agreement to carry on. The therapist has responsibility for setting out the contract that governs the therapeutic relationship.

THE INTAKE PROCESS IN INDEPENDENT PRACTICE

When assessing a client for his or her suitability for therapy, this assessment may need to be undertaken rapidly over the phone.

> **Therapist**: Hello.
>
> **Client**: Hi. Is that Mike Jones?
>
> **Therapist**: Yes it is. How can I help you?
>
> **Client**: I've been given your telephone number by somebody I was hoping to see but they've got no availability to see any new clients at the moment.

When a client contacts a therapist in independent practice, by phone, via e-mail or less commonly by letter, they will typically communicate a number of issues to the therapist. The first will be an indication of their distress, which is in essence their view of their issue or problem. This may be described in terms of a 'problem', a 'difficulty', an 'enquiry', an 'enquiry on behalf of someone else' or an 'enquiry about therapy generally'. These distinctions are important because at this stage the prospective client is concerned not only with your experience in working with such issues, but also with the potential nature of the therapeutic relationship and the contract that may develop from this. They are simultaneously endeavouring to articulate something about their problem, to discover the therapist's experience and competence in dealing with the problem and to seek to discover whether they are compatible with the therapist and can afford the sessions. No mean feat!

The same applies to aspects of the therapist's assessment. This is termed 'therapeutic fit' and is relevant to any and every therapeutic relationship. The client has choices about whether he or she wants to continue in a therapeutic relationship. The therapist has a duty to determine whether there is sufficient 'fit' between themselves and the client for therapy to work.

> **Therapist**: Right. Just to check – that's to see a therapist, is that right?
>
> **Client**: Well, the person I spoke to was a counsellor.
>
> **Therapist**: A counsellor. OK. Firstly, can I just check – have you got a few moments to speak? Are you free to speak now and are you in a place where you have a bit of privacy as well, just because there are a few questions I'd like to ask you first? I just want to check that I'm the right sort of person for you.

Many clients, as we know, may have preconceptions as to what happens in psychological therapy. A number may have previously seen a therapist and this experience may have afforded them an opportunity to experience therapy from one perspective. These preconceptions may include an expectation that there will be regular sessions, that these will be arranged at a similar time and that therapy will continue over a course of sessions that can last weeks, months or even years.

For other prospective clients, this may be their first foray into therapy and their uncertainty about the process and expectations of what may happen may be entirely different. It is not uncommon, for example, for some prospective clients to request particular 'brands', approaches or schools of therapy such as 'cognitive behaviour therapy' or 'analytic therapy'. This does not necessarily mean that they understand those terms. For others there may be an expectation that there will be no more than a one-off meeting that will resolve their problem, much in the same way as may happen when they attend their GP for a medical problem.

> **Client**: I'm in the office at the moment but I've got a bit of privacy to chat for a few few minutes.
>
> **Therapist**: That's great. We may need five or so minutes. It would be helpful, just so that I can understand a bit about what your needs are and so that I can try to assess whether, as I said, I would be the right person for you, because otherwise I would
>
> Ⅲ➡

> obviously want to put you in contact with a colleague who might be better able to help if that isn't to be me. Can you tell me what it was that got you in contact with this other colleague in the first instance?

The prospective client may also convey that they may be afraid or even ashamed of having their problem discussed in their first contact with you. This is an affective response and it is basic for the therapist engaging with the client in any context to convey some level of empathy and validate the client's positive step that they have taken in making contact. To this end, the therapist should affirm the client's help-seeking as much as dealing with practical and contractual issues all in a short space of time.

> **Client**: A few months ago I was made redundant and I've been unemployed, which has led to some mood and confidence issues that I'm struggling with at the moment.
>
> **Therapist**: I am sorry to hear that. OK, so just to check – you were made redundant and then this has affected your mood a bit and your self-confidence? Is this anything that you've spoken to anyone else about; perhaps your GP or another professional?
>
> **Client**: No, not as yet. I did try and be in touch with Samantha King, who gave me your number.
>
> **Therapist**: That's fine. Well done for taking this first step, it's not always easy. Is there anything else you were specifically hoping for in therapy?

The prospective client may also be concerned about how their problem is going to be dealt with. Stereotypes about therapy abound, as we know. Some prospective clients may fear that they are binding themselves into months or years of therapy and may worry that this could become emotionally gruelling and financially draining. For others, they may worry that at this point of emotional vulnerability in their life, therapy may make them feel worse about themselves by needing to 'delve deep' into their past and current situation, rendering them more distressed than before starting therapy. Most experienced therapists will be only too aware of these concerns that prospective clients may convey directly or indirectly. They may need to be addressed, even briefly, and dealt with when engaging with the client.

Some may be uncertain about and afraid of therapy. If we accept some popular stereotypes, they may wonder whether there will be a couch they are required to lie on, and whether the therapist will share any personal details about themselves in the course of therapy. Many other expectations, thoughts and fears may pass through their mind.

> **Client**: Well I suppose just to get another viewpoint as a starter and just to feel my way about . . . or finding a way of getting back on track really. Maybe get a few tools or thoughts to help me move on.
>
> **Therapist**: Okay. Have you ever met with a counsellor or therapist before?
>
> **Client**: Just once. I saw a school counsellor but that was obviously very many years ago. I've never really seen a therapist.

HOW IS THIS DIFFERENT FROM ANY OTHER SETTING FOR THERAPY?

The client's thoughts and fears may be more pressing and of a personal nature when you are working in independent practice, as they may project these onto their prospective therapist rather than onto an institution. This arises because a referral to an independent practitioner carries with it unique transferential and countertransferential processes. Direct contact with their prospective therapist, as opposed to contact via a secretary or receptionist, brings the client into immediate emotional and professional proximity with you. Each of you may project feelings or associations onto the other, and a mental image of the other starts to be created. The client's pain, distress, reticence, ambivalence, confusion or resentment and shame may be conveyed even before the two of you arrange to meet.

In independent practice, you will want to rapidly decide whether you can work with the client and/or the problem. You also have to be clear about the limits of your competence and, if necessary, 'reject' the client. They have started to engage with you, so this has to be done in a manner that is professional and not emotionally damaging to the client or to your own professional reputation if you decide that this is a person or problem you do not feel able to work with.

> **Therapist**: What I propose is that we think about having an initial meeting and in that consultation time it will give me an opportunity to learn more about you and how this situation is affecting you, and perhaps also we can think of some ideas that could be helpful to you to help you get through this time. Just a few practical things – do you have any restrictions about when you might be able to attend? I note that you're perhaps not in work at the moment. How are you fixed in the daytime?
>
> **Client**: I'm just working out my notice period at the moment but within a week I'll probably be free all day, any day.
>
> **Therapist**: OK, so maybe we can look to the end of that time and when you're a bit freer because I find that my daytime sessions tend to be a little bit easier at this time of year. There are a few other things. Firstly, I work in the Islington area of London. I don't know where you are currently working, or more importantly perhaps, where you live?
>
> **Client**: I live in Camden so it's not too far.

Most referrals to an independent practitioner may also carry with them particular expectations for the client. For example, a friend or colleague of the prospective client may have said, 'You must see Jane: she is such a warm and supportive person and she will be perfect for you during this time of your bereavement', 'Sophie is a highly experienced cognitive analytic therapist' or 'I know that Steven has helped lots of people who have a fear of spiders. He has an amazing reputation helping people who have phobias.' There may be something intensely personal about a referral to an independent practitioner and the client's projections and expectations and whole demeanour can, in some respects, be flattering. The therapist can also be left feeling uncomfortable or constrained in how they proceed with the client. Unless the prospective client has found your name through a therapy website or has been referred through another source where your personal credentials may be less well known, such projections and expectations are not always welcome or straightforward.

The client will, of course, be curious or anxious to know from you whether you can help them with their problem. This is something that they may wish to discuss with you over the telephone before coming to see you. This aspect of the intake may differ from that of the NHS, for example, where client choice over their therapist may be either limited or non-existent. The reason is that the prospective client may seek some level of engagement with you in order to determine whether they *feel* some level of fit between themselves and you as a practitioner. They may pose questions about your experience, qualifications, competency and interest in a particular problem.

At first, these may seem impertinent or challenging. Some questions may be specific and of a more personal nature, such as wishing to know your age, relationship status, whether you are a parent, apart from other details such as where you practise from and your consultation fee. For a few, issues relating to the gender of the therapist may also be relevant even though this is not expressed directly. The client may convey this through their hesitancy, distancing and excessive caution or persistence.

While many of these issues may be relevant to therapy in general, they may be especially important when working in independent practice and prompt you to be more willing to openly discuss these issues in a more direct manner, in a way that you would not normally discuss with clients seen in other settings. It is also important to do so in a protracted time-frame. You will want to guard against starting therapy in a formal sense over the phone or via e-mail, while the prospective client seeks seemingly endless detailed information about therapy and the therapist under the guise of working out whether to arrange a consultation, when their persistence may really amount to the start of therapy but over the phone.

The client who produces new questions and quizzes you extensively (and subjectively, from the therapist's perspective, to an excessive extent) could be either invited to attend a first session in order to further explore their issues or concerns about therapy and/or the therapist, or politely encouraged to reflect on their motivation for therapy at this time if this appears to reflect their ambivalence.

Their uncertainty could also be positively interpreted as 'caution'. You may wish to encourage them to reflect on their motivation or even to contact another therapist to see whether their doubts and uncertainties are better addressed by them, if this persists.

Client: Well, as I said, I've just been made redundant so while I feel I need to deal with this matter urgently, I also have limited funds. I'm also on the company medical scheme for another month after my redundancy so I don't know whether they will be in a position to contribute anything.

Therapist: OK, so maybe that's something that you might check and then get back to me and we can see if that would work. Sessions are fifty minutes, just short of an hour; most therapists

⦀➡

work in that timeframe. When we meet up, if that's what you decide, you'll notice that we have a very interactive session. There's a lot that happens: time to share your thoughts and feelings, opportunity for me to learn more about your issues and I would also like to help you to feel better after our first meeting. There may be some practical ideas to help you. I'm going to try and do the most in the shortest possible time, to make our time together worthwhile for you and also so that you feel that you start to benefit quite quickly as well. Is there anything else that you need to know about in terms of how I work or how things proceed from here and so on?

Client: Yes, I was wondering whether you've dealt with mood issues before and confidence matters.

Therapist: Sure, I appreciate you asking that. The answer is yes, very much. It is a surprisingly common issue that affects many people in many different ways as you can imagine, and for many different reasons. But yes, I do feel confident in dealing with confidence issues and those relating to mood.

Client: Can you give me some sort of idea of what I might expect after a set number of meetings, what I can hope to achieve?

Therapist: Obviously I'd like to say to you exactly how things are going to progress, but that's difficult, especially before a first session. I can give you an idea of what I imagine could happen. In the first meeting, as I said, I would need to learn a lot more about you and your situation. About your work; how work came to an end; how you're feeling about it; what other skills you have; how this affects your mood and people around you; what's going on in your relationships and so on. And also to think a bit about any skills that may be needed for you to move on in your life. Sometimes just a few meetings may be sufficient for this.

FORMING A CONTRACT

The formal part of the relationship with the client is known as the contract, and the more practical aspects are considered in a later chapter. It is based on many different factors. The first is trust. The client should reasonably expect you to conduct yourself in a professional manner at all times. This includes taking the initiative to discuss and form the contract. This also includes discussion about when sessions are held, how long they will last, broadly what will be covered in sessions, the nature and limits of confidentiality, your fee, as well as payment terms and other practical matters such as your cancellation policy.

> **Therapist**: Let's look at a diary and see if we can fit in a time, if that's what you would like to do. Just one other issue – if we fix up a time, I do very much appreciate being informed twenty-four hours in advance if there is a reason why you can't keep this appointment, just so that I can then allocate the time to someone else. Otherwise, there may be a charge for missing the appointment, unless you are too ill to attend. You do have my phone number and this is always a good way to reach me. You may get through to my answering machine if I am busy, but I do try to return messages within the hour. Anything else, just before we end here?
>
> **Client**: No, I think that's about it for now. I look forward to getting in touch with you to fix up a date for an appointment.
>
> **Therapist**: That's fine. By the way, just before we sign off, do you have an e-mail address because I'd like to pop a note to you reminding you about the terms that I follow in my practice and this could be helpful for you to look at in advance. It also gives a map to my consulting room and explains a few other details and tells you a little bit more about me, if that's of interest.
>
> **Client**: Sure, my e-mail address is . . .

Trust underpins the professional therapy relationship and is the basis on which your reputation is enhanced. A professional who is regarded as untrustworthy may be less likely to receive new referrals, and can do damage to how others view the profession. Trust goes hand in hand with good ethical practice and reputation. It is vital that a practitioner working in independent practice puts the issue of trust and good ethical practice to the forefront of how they relate to clients and other professionals.

Our professional standing is arguably under closer scrutiny in independent practice and colleagues will rightly make judgements about your character, professionalism and standards of practice based on your actions more than on your web page design or even your qualifications. Your last session with a client reflects your current standards of professionalism.

Paperwork can seem burdensome in independent professional practice but good record keeping can also protect the professional relationship between you and your client. Paperwork can include a client registration form, a contract that is signed by both practitioner and client, record keeping of sessions, copies of documents or letters sent to other professionals and records of any psychological questionnaires or tests that the client completes.

All therapists are accountable for their conduct in practice. Therapist accountability is firstly to the client. Nothing must ever be done in the course of therapy that will physically or psychologically harm the client. There must never be deceit, either by omission or as an intended action in order to conceal something from the client. An example of this may be in relation to your fee: the client should know what this will be in advance and there should be no possibility for misunderstandings. Since the highest standards of professionalism must be observed at all times it is advisable not to engage with a client where this may be compromised.

The contract should also state your cancellation policy. This may seem obvious, but in independent practice, the client may not fully understand or appreciate this and other components of the contract, including whether and how they can contact you, if needed, between sessions.

Each code of practice that governs psychologists, counsellors and psychotherapists stipulates that we must practise within our limits of competence. It is seen as good practice to refer clients to more competent colleagues should your client's problems exceed your capabilities. To persist with a client when we are unable to help them is unprofessional. You are also more likely to enhance your professional relationship with your client and with colleagues if your limits are acknowledged and respected.

There are legal considerations to forming a contract. A contract is an agreement between two or more competent parties in which an offer is made and is accepted. This agreement can be formal, informal, written or oral. Some are required to be in writing in order to be enforced. This is especially relevant to those pertaining to financial matters. Interestingly, it is not a legal requirement to have a written contract with a client. Nonetheless, it is considered good practice to do so and the effect will be to reduce possible misunderstandings, challenges or even accusations being levelled, which could be damaging to the therapeutic relationship and to your reputation.

An agreement between two parties creates obligations to do something (or not do so) that is the subject of the agreement. This 'binds' people together. The contract protects the therapeutic relationship and both client and therapist should have the contract as a reference point should they need to revisit it. Clarity and simplicity in a contract may be especially relevant when the client is in emotional distress. For example, clients who are severely depressed or anxious may forget or misinterpret information that is exchanged between themselves and the therapist. In order to prevent this from happening, the essential aspects of the contract should always be put in writing and also expressed in plain language. It may be helpful in some cases to allow the client some time to reconsider and reflect on the contract if they are in any way uncertain or distressed emotionally. For example, you could give the client a written contract that begins with the statement below

> Now that we have had an opportunity to meet and talk about the issue you wish to explore, you may need to go away and think about whether you want to set up any further appointments, or you may have already made up your mind. If you choose to continue, it may be helpful to have some of the practical aspects of our contract written down.

In order for a contract to be valid, it must be by the mutual assent of two parties, in this case the client and the therapist. But it could also be a couple or family; in the latter case, the contract should still be with one competent adult member. The client must be mentally competent to be able to enter into a contract. This is important in terms of the client's mental state. For example, a client who is deemed to be severely mentally ill or psychotic may not be competent to enter into a contract. It is the therapist's task and duty when working independently to determine this before asking the client to enter into a contract. This is one reason why many therapists who work independently choose not to work with severely mentally ill clients. However, should a client become severely mentally ill during the course of therapy, it may be advisable to suspend the contract and refer the client to more specialist help, such as the client's GP or specialist psychiatrist, until therapy can resume.

Finally, whatever is exchanged between client and therapist, or agreed upon, must be legal. Therefore, there can be no question of anything fraudulent, immoral or contrary to professional ethics being agreed upon. It is unacceptable and unethical, for example, for a practitioner to exchange services. The therapist cannot ask a builder who attends for therapy to come and build a wall in exchange for services. The disciplinary notices in most professional therapy magazines provide real instances of disciplinary proceedings brought against colleagues. Most reflect poor contracting and avoidable misunderstandings, poor levels of supervision and transgressions of professional boundaries and poor levels of paper-work and records in the client file.

ASSESSMENT FOR THERAPY IN INDEPENDENT PRACTICE

Assessment of client suitability for therapy in independent practice is a two-way process. It is necessary for the therapist to establish whether he or she can work with the client, as much as for the client to determine whether he or she wants to be seen and helped by you. This is in contrast to working in an organization, such as the NHS, where the choices for both the client and therapist as to who sees whom may be minimal, if they exist at all.

Failure on the part of the therapist to undertake such an assessment could be potentially damaging to your reputation if the relationship fails, and risky to physical and/or emotional safety, particularly if seeing the client in one's home. Working in independent practice may require you to make a rapid professional judgement as to whether you can work with the client and a preliminary assessment of this may need to be undertaken before a face-to-face session with the client. It may sometimes be too late to terminate with a client after a first meeting if this is the first and only context in which the client's suitability for therapy is assessed.

A client's suitability for therapy in independent practice can be determined in several ways:

- consideration of a referral form from a professional colleague (e.g. GP, psychiatrist, EAP caseworker);
- telephone or Skype contact with the prospective client to discuss their needs and to help make some assessment as to whether you feel that you can work with the client in a face-to-face session;
- e-mail contact, as above, although this can limit the amount of information that you can glean from the prospective client in the absence of verbal communication and direct interaction;
- previous clinical contact with a client who may be seeking further sessions for the same or an unrelated problem or issue.

AIMS OF ASSESSMENT

Among your first aims for assessment may be to find out whether the client:

- wants to use therapy to overcome a problem or to explore wider issues;
- is able to co-establish with the therapist general or specific and attainable goals for the therapy;

■ has realistic expectations of both therapy in general and the therapeutic relationship specifically.

You also need to consider whether the client's problem is an appropriate one for therapy and whether you feel that you can work with the client. This is where your clinical experience and intuition come into play. A referral from another practitioner may not always provide sufficient information with regard to these important aspects of the assessment. Therapists working in independent practice should probably not rely solely on the referrer's assessment of client suitability for therapy with him or her. This should always finally be determined by you! An understanding of and sound training in psychiatrically defined categories of mental health problems are desirable when working in independent practice. The reason is that this affords you insights into the nature and presentation of mental health difficulties and specific disorders and their treatment. Treatment of some of these disorders may not be compatible with your skills, expertise and experience or difficult to work with in independent practice and outside of a multidisciplinary team. Some psychological difficulties might require the intervention and expertise of other professionals alongside your therapeutic work with the client, while certain psychological disorders may be better contained within an organizational or institutional setting. There is an inherent danger for a therapist who is eager to build up their private practice to put commercial need above clinical experience and interpretive skills, to try to work with clients whose mental health difficulties may be complex and severe, and require more specialist help. While knowledge of psychiatric syndromes and problems is highly desirable, this does not mean that you work within the medical model. You may, nonetheless, be required by medical health insurers or other agencies to recognize and work within psychiatrically recognized terminology for the psychological problems that you treat. Many medical practitioners may choose to refer clients using traditional psychiatric diagnoses in their referral. These may be set out in a referral note, or the prospective client may have 'self-diagnosed' based on discussions with a professional or accessing the Internet with regard to their problem. While DSM-IV (Diagnostic and Statistical Manual for Mental Disorders) and ICD-10 (International Classification of Diseases and Related Health Problems) categorizations may alert you to possible problems the client may experience or display, these taxonomies may be of only partial value to the therapist working independently. Medical model categorizations give little guidance on how to engage with the client and give scant clues as to the client's motivation to overcome their problem. They offer only limited insight into how the individual relates to and engages with people and ideas. There is also unlikely to be insight as to how they feel about their problem, their unique attributes and limitations, the potential impact the problem has on the client's relationships with others and their self-identity, as well as the relevance of social class, gender, culture, sexual orientation and other demographics to the onset and maintenance of the problem. There are also potentially transgenerational family patterns relative to the 'cause' and maintenance of their problem, and to overcoming it. The client's core beliefs and narratives about himself or herself, the problem and therapy itself and its role in his or her life at this particular time are also relevant but not conveyed through medical diagnoses. All of these circumstances may be useful in assessing the client's suitability for therapy more holistically and for engaging positively with you (Miller, 2006). We are increasingly taught to generate a working 'formulation' of the client's problem, taking into account many different aspects of the client's problem, the context, cause or trigger of their problem, as well as what may maintain it (Corrie & Lane, 2006).

WHEN IT IS UNWISE TO ENTER A CONTRACT AS AN INDEPENDENT PRACTITIONER

The following six common problems may contraindicate seeing a client for private therapy, although specific cases should always be discussed with your supervisor.

1. Those clients whose mental or physical health state prevents them from engaging in a therapeutic relationship generally and from comprehending the questions that therapists may pose to them specifically, and who are unlikely to benefit from any therapy while these problems are evident.
2. Those who are not free to enter into a therapeutic relationship, such as clients who are coerced by a friend or relative into attending therapy. This is not to suggest that therapy cannot work with such clients, but their own motivation for therapy must be expressed, as otherwise a conflict over the aims of therapy may emerge.
3. Clients who have no real motivation to change, who simply do not want to be in therapy or who have no particular purpose or goal. Typically, these are clients who may not be genuine about seeking help but instead come to use therapy as a way of justifying why they

should not change. The initial stages of therapy can be devoted to an exploration of the client's needs and motivation for therapy. If, however, these remain unclear (apart from the context of therapy that is 'explorative', a means to 'self development and personal growth'), then there is a risk that the client will come to complain that therapy has been unhelpful or wasteful, possibly leading to a complaint against you.

4. Those whose expectations and previous experience of therapy are rigid or who are not open to different approaches to therapy and therefore should seek a different therapist or approach to therapy. This can usually be determined in an explorative intake session with the client or over the telephone before seeing them. For example, you could ask the client if they have previously seen a therapist and how they benefited from that experience.

5. Clients who cannot relate or engage in therapeutic conversation. This includes those whose cultural or national background is so different to yours that it precludes you from understanding them and vice versa.

6. In any situation in which you feel that your safety would be compromised, you should not see that client in independent practice.

A client who has been diagnosed with psychiatric illness is not necessarily unsuitable for treating in your independent practice. It is, however, important to understand the nature of their mental health problem, the extent to which it affects them, the support they receive from other professionals (such as a treating psychiatrist, GP or psychologist) and whether their specific problem might adversely affect how they relate to you in therapy. A further consideration is one pertaining to safety. While aspects of the latter are covered in some other chapters, it is helpful to re-emphasize that safety, for both the client and the therapist, is of paramount importance when working independently as a therapist.

Therapists in independent practice may not have direct and immediate access to other colleagues who can offer support or intervene should a client's behaviour become unpredictable or threatening. There may also be problems relating to the nature and extent of attachment, as well as direct access to your personal world. Some aspects of this may be impossible to keep from your client. If you see a client in your own home, the client will have some notion of how and where you live. It is not unheard of for a client who becomes distressed, uncontained or disgruntled or whose mental state deteriorates to harass a therapist even when the therapeutic relationship has ended, and this possibility and threat needs to be kept in mind before the start of psychological counselling. Safety is paramount!

CONCLUSION

For independent practitioners, it is essential to engage with the client from the first point of enquiry, as there is no organizational shield. In this chapter, we have considered how we can do that, and also explored how we can make reliable and speedy assessments of whether we are suitable for the client and vice versa.

Further guidance on how to engage with a new client and to do so in an intensive, interactive way is set out in a recent book that readers may wish to consult (Bor et al., 2004). The questions below can be used to help you reflect on how you will engage with the process.

Reflexive Points

- What are the main points you wish to elicit from a prospective client when they make a first contact with you?
- What is specific information you wish to ensure you give a prospective client?
- Do you have any 'warning bells' that may alert you to possible problems with contracting with a client: for example, issues you do not wish to work with, or signs that suggest to you that you will not be able to forge a working alliance with this person?
- If you do not feel that this is a suitable referral for you, do you have ways of saying this to clients that do not leave them feeling rejected?

Chapter 8

Marketing Your Independent Practice

INTRODUCTION

There is a possibility that some practitioners will skip over this chapter, thinking that marketing is something rather nasty and commercial, and nothing to do with a therapeutic practice. However, you do need clients and you need to keep working on this aspect of your business. So read on. We are going to intersperse the text with comments from Belinda, a colleague of ours, who was very sceptical about marketing, and asked us some pertinent questions.

> **Belinda**: OK, what exactly do you mean by marketing? Isn't it just a posh word for selling?

WHAT IS MARKETING?

In many minds, marketing is to do with the 'hard sell' or 'cold calling'. This is not the case, and there is a difference between selling and marketing. One helpful definition we have heard is that selling is about obtaining a once-off exchange, and marketing is about a relationship between the person offering the product and someone wishing to buy. For those in the helping professions, the inclusion of the word relationship can make a huge difference. In commercial terms, it also underlines another aspect of marketing – a relationship is ongoing and may include repeat business. Even if this particular contract may seem like a one-off, it is important to remember that clients may recommend you to other people, or indeed contemplate using your services again at some time in the future.

Marketing is simply about telling people what you do, communicating clearly and well, not making false claims and getting your message across to the right group of people who might wish to buy your services. As Jones (2009b) states, it is about one thing in the therapeutic world – clients. It is a way of enabling clients to assess whether you can provide what they need, whether these are individuals who may come to you directly, or providers who may have the power to buy in your services for their own clients.

If you are buying a washing machine, a car or even a new shirt, you look around, assessing whether a particular product will fit your need. Surely, this is even more important when the 'product' concerns mental and emotional well-being. As practitioners, we often talk about the need to educate clients, so that they make informed choices, and do not simply pick a therapist randomly. If we seriously believe this, we need to consider how clients can make that choice, and not just pay lip service to the *idea* of choice. Clients (or we could call them customers in this case) are often people who normally do make informed choices, so why should this not also apply to our services?

In order to establish and maintain a professional independent practice, you do need to understand market forces, while not being seduced by them solely to provide the largest income possible. If you do ignore this area, at worst, your business will fail, or grow too slowly for you to attain a reasonable income. Yet most training courses for therapists ignore this aspect of our working lives. An exception was the (now defunct) Diploma in Counselling at Work at Bristol University, where in the mid-1990s Anne Scoular presented a workshop on Marketing for Counsellors and Therapists. She maintained that our training in communication skills gives us a very good range of tools to use when marketing our practices. It is food for thought that many of our basic skills have something in common with those of successful marketers!

Having made the case for independent practitioners to consider how they market themselves and their business, the rest of this chapter is concerned with various aspects that need to be considered.

> **Belinda**: Hmmm. I am still not sure about all this marketing nonsense. I just want to get on with working with clients. All this focus on promoting myself doesn't feel as if it fits with my values as a counsellor. Is it ethical?

ETHICAL CONSIDERATIONS

As mentioned above, your marketing does need to reflect precisely what you can actually provide. There is a temptation to include anything and everything, but if you have any doubts about whether you can actually work well with couples, for example, leave that area alone, until you feel more confident or have undertaken further training. Beware of your shadow side, and avoid getting caught up in unethical marketing.

However, according to Jones (2009b), the reticence of practitioners to market themselves is potentially unethical in itself. There are misconceptions about what our professions can offer, and if we do not challenge these through appropriate marketing, we allow untrained and inferior practitioners to flourish.

Be aware that in setting up in independent practice, you are putting yourself in direct competition with other colleagues and friends who provide the same or similar services. This may be a difficult notion to acknowledge, as Thistle (1998) points out. So consider this when planning your marketing activities. Will your competitors (your colleagues) see what you are doing as ethical? Can you face them without any doubts in your mind?

Although you are unlikely to knowingly market yourself unethically, think about any advice or constraints that your professional organization may place on you, particularly in the area of advertising. Carefully scrutinize guidelines, codes of practice and ethical frameworks to ensure that you are not bringing the profession into disrepute in the eyes of the organization. If in doubt, check it out with them. You may also be constrained in the way that you describe yourself. For example, professional bodies have clear guidelines about terminology, or letters after your name – MBACP, HCP, BPS, UKCP etc. Do not imply that you are a registered or accredited member of your profession if you are not. This may seem so obvious that it is not worth mentioning, but these mistakes can occur, particularly if someone is aiding us in our marketing without knowledge and understanding of the finer details of our professional life.

Finally, if you still have some doubts in your mind about whether or not it is ethical to market yourself at all, look at those products or charities that you consider ethical. How do they go about promoting themselves, and are there any of their ways of communicating with the public that you could adopt, albeit on a smaller scale. If something specific does not sit right with you and your ethical values, try a different way of marketing yourself, rather than giving up on marketing.

> **Belinda**: I can see that it makes sense to make sure it fits with me, but how do I know what I *do* want to market?

DETERMINING WHAT YOU ARE MARKETING

The short answer to 'what are you marketing?' is yourself and your services, but that does not get you very far. First, consider how you want to present yourself, what specifically you are marketing and whom you want to target. This may lead you to realize that you may need more than one marketing avenue and differing sets of marketing tools for different audiences. For example, when approaching companies or large organizations, you might want to present as business focused, while if you are targeting individual clients, you might want a more informal, user-friendly style, while remaining professional.

List all the different areas in which you would like to work. We have mentioned most of these already, but to remind you, these might include:

- individual therapy with private clients;
- EAP clients and other company funded clients;
- NHS clients;
- couple or family work;
- specialist areas such as abuse or addiction;
- low-cost or free clients;
- therapy or supervision for trainees;
- assessments;
- supervision;
- running workshops and working with training organizations;
- mentoring and coaching.

Use this list to add and subtract your own areas of preference. It will help you to gain a clearer idea of what you want to market. Then, if you can, break your list into bundles of areas that could fit together. There will be some overlap, with some areas appearing in more than one section, as you can see in Figure 8.1.

> **Belinda**: Hold on; there's far too much here for me to do to start with. It's overwhelming.

1. Individual private clients Low-cost or free clients Couple and family work Specialist areas Trainees Medico legal	**2.** EAPs Companies Assessments
3. NHS Specialist areas Assessments	**4.** Training Teaching Workshops Therapy or supervision for trainees
5. Supervision Trainees Non-clinical: writing/publishing External examining	**6.** Mentoring Coaching Companies

Figure 8.1   Bundling your marketing areas.

A dilemma arises here: there is a need to find a focus or identity in order to gain confidence and help with the marketing process, but you also need to spread the risk and diversity to improve the range of client contracts who may access your business and for you to enjoy what you do. However, when you have done this exercise, you can see both where you might want to concentrate your energy initially, and where you need to think about different strategies for marketing your services. You might decide that for the first six months of establishing your business, you wish to attract private clients and supervisees to your practice, and therefore you will focus on boxes 1 and 5 primarily. You can then add other boxes when you feel ready to do so.

On the other hand, entering the training field as part of an established course might seem more attractive as a way of ensuring some regular income at the outset. A few brave souls will decide that in the quieter early days they will tackle all the areas they want to work in. This could pay off, or could mean that you are running around like the proverbial headless chicken. Also be aware that if you secure work to provide training in interpersonal skills for the employees of an organization, for example, this may well lead to enquiries about other things you might do. Be ready to promote your other skills and receive enquiries. Always have your business card with you to hand out. It is better to target specifically initially than be seen as offering anything and everything. Those buying your services may not have the time or inclination to discover what specifically you are able to do.

TRADING STYLE AND IMAGE

You need to make some early decisions about your corporate image – a rather grandiose way of saying that it is useful to think about the things you may want to keep on all your marketing materials.

> **Belinda**: Corporate image! It's only me you're talking about, not a corporation! I just want to know what to call my business.

Some people prefer to use their own names, while others prefer to use a company name. You could be Jo Steele, Jo Steele Therapy Services or Wellbeing Therapy. If you choose a descriptor rather than your name, take time to think about what it says, and try it out with others who will give you a frank opinion. Choosing something unusual may make people notice your materials, but will it tell them what you do? Meerkat Ltd might symbolize something for you, but will anyone else give more than a passing glance at the name and your cute picture of a meercat? Also think about how people will access you if they do an online search – by your name, through the name of your service or through the services you provide. You can check names and register your own through http://www.nominet.org.uk

You also have to decide whether your company name should include a word like 'therapy', as this could limit you when targeting some potential customers. On the other hand, such words may help the receiver to know exactly what you are offering. If you wish to have a specific name, you could register it at Companies House, to help prevent other people using it. All limited companies in England, Wales, Northern Ireland and Scotland are registered at Companies House. As their website states, the main functions of Companies House are to:

- incorporate and dissolve limited companies;
- examine and store company information delivered under the Companies Act and related legislation;
- make this information available to the public.

You can obtain more information by contacting Companies House at http://www.companieshouse.gov.uk or talk to your accountant about the possible benefits of registering, and any problems this might cause you.

Other style decisions include logos and colours. A logo can make your materials stand out, though our advice would be to choose something that is relatively simple and straightforward to reproduce. However, it should not be hand drawn or amateurish either. Again, try designs out before committing yourself, as changing headed notepaper and business cards can be costly.

Colour is very much a matter of personal taste. The golden rule is to choose a colour or colours that you like, while remembering that it also has to appeal to as large an audience as possible. Often for reproduction purposes, a pale colour, or even white, is best for the background. Keep stronger colours for your logo or to highlight something. An exception might be leaflets that you are going to leave in such places as a GP surgery waiting area or a library. Then you do want them to stand out and attract interest, though not appear lurid.

The other image consideration is about what you wear. If you are dealing with companies and large organizations, it is worth presenting a businesslike appearance, unless you happen to know that they favour a casual style. It is better to be overdressed than underdressed. In other places, such as training institutions, a smart casual style would probably be more in keeping. How you dress when with clients is unlikely to cause you angst, as you will have found your personal style in the past.

The words you use all convey a meaning and create a sense of you as a practitioner. If you look back at the various marketing areas you determined in the section above, you will realize that 'one wording will not fit all'. You have to design marketing materials to suit their purpose. Your ideal wording should reveal you as professional, avoid spectacular claims that suggest you are better or more effective than anyone else, and present your unique selling points. The use of the first person is effective and it begins to build a picture of yourself, so do not be afraid to say 'I can offer . . .' etc. You may have to be a man/woman of several hats or identities, although your core skills identity may remain the same.

> **Belinda**: I've actually done some work since we last spoke, and I have to admit that I have quite enjoyed doing all this. But I still don't like the words 'corporate image'.

USE OF OTHER PROFESSIONALS

It can be daunting to think about how to market yourself, but with some exceptions, it is often better to avoid spending vast sums of money on the services of other professionals to help you. Some exceptions might be:

- Using a printing service for your business stationery, leaflets and business cards. If you are going to do this yourself, make sure that you use high quality paper or card, that your printer is up to the job, and that if you need to make bi- or tri-folded leaflets, their final appearance is crisp.
- Employing a web designer. If you are terrified of technology, then this can be a cost effective solution. However, *you* need to keep control of the finished website by inputting your needs clearly as it is being designed. Many all-singing, all-dancing websites do not actually bring about results. The most important thing is whether it says what you want and whether prospective clients can use it easily. You can download helpful and straightforward packages to help you design your own websites, and many of these are free. If you are going to employ a web design company, ask to see other sites it has created, and find out which companies colleagues have used.

> **Belinda**: If you're reasonably good on the computer, you can certainly do this yourself. But I do think that I'll need to ask friends to look at it and give me feedback before I go live.

Unless you intend to create a huge independent practice, employing other people, you are very unlikely to need the services of a marketing company. Of course, if you number a marketer among your friends, then cultivate that friendship! You probably already have a network of friends and professional colleagues who will be willing to look at your marketing materials and give you feedback.

PROMOTING YOURSELF

So far, we have looked at marketing mainly in terms of materials and the services that you might wish to offer. This is only half the story. You need to promote yourself on all possible occasions. If reading that makes you think of overbearing people who cannot stop telling you about themselves and how good they are, think again. That is not what we mean.

Instead, we are suggesting that you are proactive and overcome any reluctance to talk about what you do. There are many opportunities to do this. First, we examine those at a macro level.

Advertise

■ Use carefully targeted advertisements. There is a very low return on such things as leaflets through doors, so do not waste time on this, unless you are promoting a workshop in a particular locality, for example. Professional journals may seem the obvious place to advertise, but it depends who you are trying to attract – clients do not often read your professional journal, though some referrers, potential supervisees and workshop attendees might.

■ Advertise in professional directories, as often potential clients recognize that there will be more safety in approaching someone listed there than from an advertisement in a paper. One problem is that not all potential clients know that such directories exist.

■ Consider whether you will put an entry into directories such as Yellow Pages. This can be very successful, though if you are on a border between two geographical areas of directories, unless you place an entry in both, it may not bring in clients. Some of the professional bodies, such as BACP, BPS and UKCP, run block advertisements for accredited members, and this may be a better (and cheaper) option than your individual entry.

You will need to weigh up the pros and cons of professional directories, paper directories and online directories such as yell.com. Most of us have a limited budget for advertising, so we do need to think this through carefully. Personally, we have found that professional directories (both online and paper) and local area Yellow Pages have worked best for us.

Raising your profile

■ Offer to give a seminar to GPs, schools, organizations or even the local Women's Institute, though there you might call it a talk rather than a seminar.

■ Publish in your professional journals, or write articles for local newspapers. These can be kept to circulate to potential referrers where appropriate.

■ If you have the necessary expertise and confidence, give media interviews. Several professional organizations offer media training workshops, which are useful in helping you to avoid the pitfalls and get across your message.

Link with others

- Link with other services to present yourself as a 'whole' and also reduce your costs.
- Link with other therapists, highlighting your specialism.

Use all your skills

- Expand your repertoire into areas that use similar skills. Coaching and mentoring are good examples.
- Make use areas of expertise from a previous career, and link these to your current practice. If you worked in a large company, then you may be well placed to mentor employees now.

Don't ignore opportunities

- Listen to people you meet 'casually' as they could be useful contacts. Even the person you get into conversation with on a train that is delayed may turn out to be a contact.
- Be prepared to talk about what you do concisely and in an interesting way when you meet possible referrers at workshops, meetings or even parties.
- Always have a business card to hand.

At the micro level

- Always use headed notepaper when writing to a referrer or a client, and make sure you respond efficiently. This may not consciously register with the receiver, but if you do not do this, it will almost certainly be noticed.
- Where it would not breach confidentiality, be prepared to talk to other professionals about a client. If you unnecessarily guard anonymity, you will be perceived as unhelpful, and not register as a potential practitioner for future referrals. If it would breach professional guidelines, explain this courteously and in a friendly way.
- When talking to others, avoid psychobabble and jargon, unless you are sure they understand your meaning. It puts people off very quickly.

■ If you are contacted by someone, but you cannot help them yourself, be friendly, professional and, if you can, suggest alternative contacts. Then when there is an opening for something you can provide, the person you have given help to is much more likely to remember you, or pass your name on to someone else.

> **Belinda**: I can see that it makes sense to use opportunities. I also think that I will need to do this carefully, as I don't want to become a bore. Like I said about other things, it's got to feel right and fit with me. And there will be times when I don't feel like using the opportunity, and that's got to be OK too.

MAKING USE OF THE INTERNET

Websites

We mentioned websites above, and certainly the majority of practitioners setting up in independent practice in the twenty-first century would not dream of disregarding the marketing opportunities that a well designed website offers. As more and more people use search engines to source goods and services, therapists need to be able to be found. Even your excellent website will not ensure clients by itself. If you Google either of our names, you will get a good number of listings. The same is probably true of you; while writing this chapter, we searched for a number of fellow practitioners and could find most of them easily. However, that's not a lot of help, as most potential clients will not know your name.

So think about how you can make your site appear near the top of the lists. One useful way is to become part of an online directory such as www.counselling-directory.org.uk. Such directories will almost certainly appear on the first page of a search. Of course, they are going to list your competitors as well, but that is where your unique selling points may attract potential clients. It is pointless and costly joining directories willy-nilly. Spend time looking at the various possibilities; compare the costs of joining them; ask therapists in them how many clients actually come from these sources; decide whether the image of the directory fits with the way you want to portray yourself. Finally, it may not be wise to tie yourself in to one directory too quickly. There are often introductory offers if you sign up in advance for a longer period. However, if you find that it is not bringing in the work you want, it could prove to have been a costly mistake.

Social networking

Sometimes also known as social media, social networking refers to a variety of websites where you can have an online presence. They include many which have become part of our language: blogs, Twitter, wiki's, YouTube are all words that pepper many a conversation. Seen originally as the domain of the young, they quickly became a way of communicating for all ages at every level of society. People love them or hate them. For therapists, there are a number of advantages, and also areas where we need to think very carefully before we use social networking sites.

Mieke Haveman, a student on the General Certificate in Online Counselling (run by Online Training Limited), produced an interesting presentation on social networking in her final portfolio. She has kindly allowed two of her slides to be reproduced here.

What can they do for you?
- Give you an online presence.
- More chances to be found by search engines.
- More opportunities to express yourself and show more than you can on your professional website (blog).
- Interact with other professionals (Linkedin).
- Free publicity (fan pages on Facebook etc.).
- Link all your websites together. One message gets shown on for example Facebook, Linkedin and Twitter (Hootsuite).

Mieke Haveman: www.safehavencoaching.eu (OLT 2010)

Pitfalls
- Social media are NOT private. Set BOUNDARIES.
- Clients can read your blogs.
- On Facebook/Linkedin think carefully whom you add as friends.
- Make sure you have privacy settings in place on sites if you don't want clients to read your comments.
- Everybody who wants to can follow Twitter, you cannot prevent people befriending you.
- Be careful with the photos you place online. On Facebook, for example, they become property of Facebook.
- What you put on the Internet stays there forever and cannot be deleted.

Mieke Haveman: www.safehavencoaching.eu (OLT 2010)

So there are some very compelling reasons for considering using social networking sites. However, during the course, Mieke realized that there were various problems with using these as frequently, or in the same way, as she had been doing, now that she was also becoming an independent practitioner. Because they have limited privacy, there is a huge need to reflect on what you post. Hence the slide above on the pitfalls. Don't dismiss them, but go in with eyes wide open.

APPLYING MARKETING THEORIES

While as an independent practitioner it is unlikely that you are going to make use of the marketing theories and strategies that larger organizations use, there are a few that it might be helpful to consider.

The first is unique selling point or USP. Consider what it is about you and your practice that is different from other practices in your area. Why should clients choose you rather than anyone else? If your answer to this is that you do not know, then potential clients may feel the same. So stop and seriously weigh up your practice. Look at the materials that other practitioners use, not just therapists but also other professional service firms such as lawyers, accountants and consultants. As Jones (2009b) suggests, they too win business based on their personal credibility to deliver value and client service. Some examples of points to consider might be:

- your years of experience – 'fifteen years working as a therapist . . .';
- the breadth of your experience – 'I have worked with a wide range of client issues including . . .';
- the range of services you can offer – 'I offer counselling, supervision, training and coaching' or 'I work with families, children and couples, as well as individual adults';
- fee considerations – 'I offer reduced fees for trainees' or 'I offer income-related fees';
- your geographical situation – 'My practice is situated close to good bus and train links' or 'There is ample parking space';
- your physical working space – 'My practice room is situated in a large Victorian house with delightful grounds';
- past work – 'I have worked with major companies, not-for-profit organizations and individuals';
- your links – 'My practice is linked to a number of other independent practitioners, providing a range of therapies including hypnotherapy, aromatherapy . . .'

- your contacts – 'I have established links with psychiatrists, psychologists, career and debt counsellors, and mediators';
- 'I can speak another language fluently enough to offer this therapeutically'.

Not all of these will be relevant, but you will have one or more USP, so find it and use it! You will want to appear professional, warm, confident and as the person to approach before anyone else.

> **Belinda**: I've never thought I might have anything that might be termed unique professionally as a counsellor. But I can see that the fact that I've worked at a senior level in a multinational might mean that some local companies might consider using me as a counsellor.

Another useful tool that you will probably have come across if you have worked in an organization in the past is a SWOT Analysis. Here you are looking at your Strengths, Weaknesses, Opportunities and Threats (see Figure 8.2).

Your own SWOT analysis will look very different, of course, but once you have done this exercise for yourself, play to your strengths and opportunities, and consider how to minimize your weaknesses and threats. For example, you could ask a trusted friend to role-play face-to-face and telephone situations with you to help you build up your confidence in how you can improve the way you come across. You could make contact with other therapists, or set aside time each week in your diary to tackle the paperwork – and do not let yourself become involved in displacement activities! Look at your outgoings ruthlessly and see if these can be reduced. Provide maps and directions for clients. Think about how to make your advertisement in the phone directory stand out from the others.

A further tool is the Boston Matrix, which is a chart created in 1970 by Bruce Henderson for the Boston Consulting Group. It is particularly useful if you have been in independent practice for a while, although it is also helpful for newer practitioners who bring skills and resources from previous employment, both as therapists and in other fields. It can be a valuable aid in deciding what you want to include in your portfolio of offerings, where to spend time and where to let go of things that will no longer increase your income. Because of the delightful terminology, it may well appeal to your creative side. The basics in the tool are shown in Figure 8.3: you add your various activities to each section.

Strengths	Weaknesses
■ I am very experienced ■ I know I come across well when meeting people for the first time ■ I already have excellent premises ■ I have made good contacts with other professionals ■ I am accredited	■ I have a tendency to underplay my strengths ■ I am not good on the telephone ■ I am not part of any network ■ I let paperwork build up ■ I find it difficult to be brief and succinct
Opportunities	Threats
■ I have a range of skills ■ A previous employer already wants me to do some work for him ■ My local newspaper runs a series on health matters, so I could contact them to offer an article on counselling ■ The local college is advertising for maternity cover on a counselling course ■ I can use micro opportunities such as copying letters to raise awareness of my name and profile ■ I circulate my powerpoint presentations to other potential 'buyers'	■ There are fifteen other therapists advertising in the phone directory ■ My premises are difficult to find ■ I only have sufficient savings to cover the first three months' outgoings

Figure 8.2   A sample SWOT analysis of Boston Matrix terminology.

Cash cows are the things that bring in a sizeable proportion of your income, and on the whole trundle along nicely without you having to do very much to ensure they happen. What these cash cows actually are will vary from individual to individual, but could include a well established contract with a training organization, EAP clients, long-term supervisees or private clients coming from a range of sources. They do need some time spent on them: for example, in keeping good contact with referrers, or making sure we know well in advance if a supervisee is going to retire or

Cash cows	**Rising** stars
Old dogs	**Problem** children

Figure 8.3 The basics of the Boston Matrix.

change supervisors, so that we can replace them. There will be ongoing costs, such as advertising. However, compared with some other aspects of your business, the time and money outlays will be minimal. They are the mainstay of our business. They may not grow much year on year, but while they may no longer generate huge excitement, as long as we are not bored by them, and therefore work less effectively and ethically, they are still central and valuable.

Old dogs are aspects of your work that have probably been cash cows, but you now need to consider whether they are actually still important parts of your work or not. Do they generate enough work and income for the outlay on them to make it worthwhile retaining them? There are a number of points to consider here. If we take as an example your work with a particular referrer, it could be that in the past you have had a large number of referrals. However, these have dropped off over the past eighteen months to a point where you are wondering if it is worth the time you spend keeping contact with the agency, and filling in their lengthy forms for the odd client. Or perhaps an EAP has not put up the fee they pay for two years, and has said that they are not going to do so in the foreseeable future. Would you do better to make contact with another EAP where you might receive a more reasonable rate for your time? If you offer training, you might have a workshop that has been highly successful in the past, but needs a major overhaul to update it now. Before you spend your time doing this, think carefully about the current market. Is what you offer still in line with areas that individuals and organizations are seeking? CPD needs and fashions change with the times.

A final word about old dogs: just like real old dogs, they can be much loved and favourite pets. While the logical sense might be to get rid of them at this point, we may decide that we love them too much, and choose to retain them. That can be our choice, as long as we have at least considered the reasons for it, and know why we are doing this.

Problem children, or question marks as they are sometimes referred to, are those parts of our work that will take a lot of time and energy, and possibly money too. It is usually a new venture that we want to undertake that has the potential to become a main part of our work. It can often be where our creative passion for developing ourselves personally and professionally will lie. Sensibly, it may also depend on seeing where trends are going and seeing if we can be part of the providing team. Be aware of where government (or other) funding is being targeted, and consider whether you have the necessary skills to be able to benefit from this. At the time of writing, practitioners are conscious that if they can offer CBT to clients, they are likely to have a better chance of NHS referrals. While some practitioners might recoil at the thought of changing their practice to suit the market, others will be aware that they already do incorporate CBT techniques and strategies into their current approach, and what they need to do is simply refocus their literature and personal approaches to potential referrers to take account of this. What you would need to consider is whether you think this trend will be long enough lasting to warrant putting effort into this area.

A slightly more problematic child could involve a decision to undertake some specific training in a new area, in order to incorporate this into your work. Think carefully about the balance of this being something you would really like to do and the work it will bring in. A sound training in couple or family work might pay off financially, as there seems to have been difficulty over a long period of time in finding referral possibilities for those seeking such therapy. So the considerable investment in time and money needed might well be worthwhile. However, undertaking training in sand tray work might be more risky. Will you be able to use it in your current practice? If not, are there sufficient new avenues of referral to make it viable? Crucially, that is not to say that we should never either undertake training or begin a new specialism simply because we are unsure that it will bring us sufficient client income. It is simply a means of knowing what our motivation is – mainly income or mainly increasing our skills and knowledge in a more general way that satisfies our creative need for development to keep us alive both professionally and personally. That way we avoid risk and disappointment if it cannot do both things.

Rising stars are those aspects of the problem children that have begun to become successful. They may be areas where we are at the forefront of developments. They may take more than an equal share of time and investment, but have the potential to become cash cows. An example would be where we have decided that training in CBT is worthwhile; we have marketed ourselves well, and are getting referrals. This could potentially become a large part of our client work.

Another area that has the potential for growth is to develop skills as an online counsellor or supervisor. Therapists who have trained in this area may find that the uptake is slow initially, but they have an eye to the future and what is happening in other parts of the world, and take the opportunity to incorporate this way of working in their portfolio (Jones & Stokes, 2009).

If you offer training, keep an eye on new developments to see where you might be able to proffer your services. Do you have expertise that could be used in a workshop? Many training courses will want to give students an opportunity to know about the newer approaches and research, but the main tutors may not have the expertise to do this. So there is a possible market there for you. The other benefit of doing this is that a wider audience will be aware of you, and what else you can provide.

Be aware though, that some rising stars never become more than that. If they are not being helpful to maintaining your independent practice, you may need to drop them before they become old dogs. Stardom to dogdom can be very rapid!

If reading about the Boston Matrix has left you wondering about whether it does connect with you and your practice, remember its aims:

- to avoid having too many new irons in the fire at any one time, so that your time, energy and capital are not eaten away;
- to enable you to be consciously aware of what brings you most satisfaction and also most income;
- to remain alert to trends and possible opportunities;
- to identify what you are doing that may undermine your growth and take steps to minimize those areas.

> **Belinda**: I can really go with this – it's taking me back into my old career, when I would hear other people using language like this. At one level, it was part of the reason I left all that behind. At another, I know it made sense! I think one of my problems has been that in retraining, I thought I was entering a profession that was pure and had no need of such things. However, I'm realizing that if I want to succeed, it might be best to not to throw the baby out with the bathwater!

CONCLUSION

Although many therapists shy away from thinking about marketing, if you want to be successful – and presumably you do or you would not have chosen to be independent – then spending some time considering what you want to do, and the best ways of doing this, is essential. All it requires is for you be brave enough to set aside thoughts of 'not being good enough' or being too self-effacing to say what you do clearly and effectively to the right people at the right time. If you do not do this, there are plenty of other perfectly reputable professionals who will do it, and they will be the ones to succeed in their independent practice.

Reflexive Points

- Make a chart that sums up your attitude to marketing – what you consider possible and what does not sit well with you professionally. Be honest as this should help to clarify in what arenas you are prepared to market yourself.
- Make a list of potential ways of promoting yourself – only include those that do not conflict with the point above.
- Carry out a SWOT analysis. Then reflect on how to use your strengths and opportunities, and minimize the weaknesses and threats.
- If you are an established practitioner, or have been employed in related areas, make your own Boston Matrix, to contemplate areas you might increase or let drop from your portfolio.

Chapter 9

Managing Risk:
Day to Day Issues

INTRODUCTION

In this chapter we will look at some of the risk areas for those in independent practice. Most practices run from home or small premises do not go bankrupt; they fail either because the practitioner can see that they are not financially viable and close their practice, or they have not taken due account of the risk areas facing them. However, if we can minimise the risks, we are then only left with our own fears and, as Nelson Mandela eloquently pointed out in his Presidential Acceptance Speech, 'Our greatest fear is not that we are inadequate. Our deepest fear is that we are powerful beyond measure. . . . As we are liberated from our own fear, our presence automatically liberates others'. That is to say, it is often our unconscious fear of being too powerful that may hold us back. We need to harness our personal power and use it effectively and ethically, rather than fear it.

As independent practitioners, we largely depend on our reputation and this can be very slow to build, though as mentioned in other parts of this book, there are things we can do to help it on its way. One of the reasons that we fear the risks of being independent is that we have nightmares about loosing our hard won reputation in one fell swoop. This is rarely so, unless we have indulged in malpractice, and many of the risks are easily avoidable if we think them through in advance.

RISKS FROM OURSELVES

Some of the risks will depend on us as individuals. It is vital that we are ruthlessly honest in knowing our own characteristics and those that will help us succeed and those that are more likely to put our business at risk. If we know that we are timid and have never been a risk taker in any aspect of our lives in the past, then peculiarly one of the greatest threats to our success is that we will avoid even acceptable risk. Conversely, if we are great risk takers, we may not give enough serious consideration to what needs to be done to minimize risks, but sail blithely into troubled waters. What we have to do is find a balance of acceptable risk taking, and have fall back possibilities in place, should we have made a wrong decision.

Another risk for independent practitioners is to see themselves as somehow 'lesser'. Never, even in your own mind, allow yourself to say 'I am *only* an independent practitioner'. If that is how you see yourself, that is what you will inevitably, though subtly, give off to other people you meet. So you are not a staff counsellor for a large multimillion international organization – so what? You are a bold pioneer, striking off on your own, facing risks and challenges, running your own business, and a successful entrepreneur. Hold onto that image in the face of risk and challenge.

It is very easy in the initial stages when our work is slow to take off, or indeed later when we seem to be stagnating a little, to become very despondent. This will impinge on our business and put it at risk. These times are inevitable in most practices, and the way forward is to be fore-warned and have coping strategies in place. These will include practical solutions to get business moving forward again as well as tactics for looking after ourselves in times of gloom, such as seeing friends, or spending time doing something we enjoy away from work.

Maria qualified two years ago and has since done her degree year. She is beginning to build up an independent practice.

> **Maria**: I'm keeping on two placements, otherwise I'd probably go stir crazy. The one thing I do find in independent practice is that it's either feast or famine. If you still have the placements, it keeps you ticking over, and you don't get into a place of thinking 'Oh my God; they're not coming because I'm not good enough.'

ASSESSING WHERE WE ARE

There is a risk in simply going on as we have always gone on. From time to time, we should step back from our work, and think about where we are aiming – is what we are currently doing still in line with where we want to get to? And just as importantly, is where we wanted to get to initially still where we want to go now? Our original plan might have been to have a solid practice made up of individual clients and supervisees. However, due to opportunities that have come our way, we now find ourselves with a more mixed portfolio of work – clients, supervisees, group work workshops, lectures, writing, training etc. Weigh up whether this is actually what you want to do, or if your passion (and possibly financial security) still lies in working with individuals. If so, then you may be at risk of losing enthusiasm for what you are engaged in, and need to pull back in declining further invitations to do other things. Passion is a major driving force in success!

On the other hand, if you realize that this mixed set of occupations is precisely what you enjoy, then look at your business plan again. Does it make sense, for example, to be renting a room for five days a week when you are only in it for three days, on average? Could you group your individual work, so you can reduce the cost of renting to three days? Perhaps you need to change your advertising strategies to reflect what you actually do, or drop some of the more costly ones targeted at bringing you individual clients.

So take the time to assess your current position. 'A man (or a woman) going nowhere usually gets there.' If you want to avoid getting nowhere, put time into periodic risk assessment. Often we do this when we begin our business, but forget to do regular reviews.

> **Carrie**: When I first began in independent practice, I thought I wanted to spend all my days with clients. The thought of being able to do just one thing, and not wear several hats, was so appealing. But now a few years later, that has changed. I missed the buzz of training and also of being with a group. So I now do quite a lot of training as well, and that gives me the best of both worlds, though it is sometimes hard to juggle.

RISK ASSESSMENT

In carrying out a risk assessment, you will need to look at various areas, and we will examine some of these in more detail below. They include:

◼ financial position (Can I afford to do this?);

- social (What impact is this having on my friends, family and lifestyle?);
- career (What impact is this having on my professional self-image, my ambition and my relationship with colleagues?);
- legal (Do I have the full range of insurances and indemnities in place? Am I sufficiently aware of how to respond to solicitor or court requests?);
- personal safety (Are there risks from where I see people or the type of issues I deal with?);
- negligence and malpractice (Have I got the right backup to ensure I do not make clinical mistakes? Have I thought about client complaints?);
- suicidal clients (How will I manage these challenging situations?).

When we talked about doing a risk assessment with colleagues, there were groans all round, until one voice piped up:

> You remember last year when I didn't see any of you for ages. Well, I suppose in a funny sort of way I was doing a risk assessment. I wouldn't have called it that at the time, but now looking back, I wish I had done this risk thing earlier. I had got to a silly stage. My friends and family never saw me. I'd take on any work that came. It was only when there was a threat of a complaint from a client that I stopped and realized that my business (and maybe my clients too) were at risk. Luckily the complaint didn't come to anything, but it might have and then where would I have been?

FINANCIAL RISKS

Chapter 5 deals with many aspects of the financial characteristics of beginning your independent practice. Here we mention some other risk areas to keep in mind. A useful newssheet on the risks of working from home was issued by Towergate (2009), one of the providers of indemnity policies for practitioners.

Home insurance

This bulletin includes the reminder that we may be putting our home insurance cover at risk, not only if we see clients at home, but also if we keep property belonging to the business there. Such things include laptops, business files, projectors etc. You will usually have insurance under your home policy for harm or injury to a visitor. This will not apply to clients.

If you have not already done so, then talk to your home insurers. Unfortunately, you may find that you have to pay a higher premium, or that some aspects of your cover are restricted. The temptation is to bury your head in the sand and do nothing, saying to yourself, 'Well, if I lose some property that belongs to my business, I'll just not claim for it.' However, it is not that simple, as failure to disclose any changes to the use of the property may also affect your claim for things not related to your work, including having it refused. If your insurer cannot provide you with work-related cover, then it is worth researching to find one that will.

Pensions

Another risk element is in providing for our future. Pension provision may seem a long way off and something that can be left until we are more secure financially. Indeed, in the financial climate at the time of writing, even those who have made wise pension provision are discovering that the sums they could confidently expect are unlikely to be realized. It is a huge temptation to cross our fingers and do nothing. However, be realistic about what you need to do. It is probably sensible to begin to build up your 'pension pot' as early as possible, even if initially you can only put small amounts into it. As you become more financially secure, you can increase your monthly outlay.

If you are in part-time employment as well as being self-employed, you are likely to be in a better position, as you can also continue to contribute to your employment pension scheme. The same applies if you are leaving paid employment and have built up what would perhaps amount to half of a full employment pension, for example. You will at least have some income from that when you reach retirement age, though unless you have been in the public sector, or in a very good company scheme, this is now unlikely to be index-linked. Therefore, while seeming reasonable at present, it may not be so in ten or twenty years time. There is a great temptation when becoming self-employed to take out a lump sum from your previous pension pot, if you are allowed to do so, to see you through the initial drop in income. Unless you find a very good way of investing this sum to give you income from the interest accrued, it may be a very short-term benefit. Weigh the options up carefully, and if necessary consult an independent financial advisor.

Thinking about your pension does not necessarily mean investing in a pension scheme. You could look at 'risk free' investment schemes. While nothing is truly risk free, since, as we have discovered, even banks can collapse, investing in something that is 'risk averse' at a reasonable rate of return over a long period can mean that you have a sizable sum when you retire, and could potentially live off the interest from it. Be prepared to take the time to look after your investment, and move it around providers who offer better rates, while keeping the risk as low as possible. The downside of providing your own nest egg in this way is that unlike savings put directly into an approved pension scheme, you will not be able to claim tax relief on the money you invest. If you invest in cash ISAs, you would qualify for tax relief on them, though the amount you can invest per year will be limited. You could combine a number of different ways of saving for the future to give you the best possible outcome. Again, it could be worth talking to an independent financial advisor.

Income tax and National Insurance liability

This is another risk area. It is easy to do the calculations and think that a certain number of clients will bring you the amount of income that you need. However, your income is going to be taxed and you will probably have to pay an income-related supplement for National Insurance contributions, in addition to the NI payment you make quarterly. (This latter contribution is most easily done through a direct debit arrangement, and covers some very basic items, such as a contribution to your state pension.)

You have to file a tax return for every financial year that you are self-employed, either on hard copy or online. When this has been processed, you will receive a statement from HMRS that tells you how much you have to pay, in two sums, during the next year. It is essential that you have kept back some of your income to cover these amounts. If you have not done so, then you risk having to take out a bank loan to pay the tax liability. It can be hard to estimate the amount you will need to put by during your first year of business, but a rough and ready guide would be that tax is unlikely to be more than 25 per cent of your income, unless you are making large amounts in this initial year. You can claim for many business expenses, including business-related postage, stationery, professional subscriptions, supervision, CPD etc.

You may wish to file your tax return yourself, or you may decide that it is worth investing in an accountant to do this for you. The advantage is that accountants know many things that can be claimed that the layperson is unaware of. The disadvantage is that you will have to pay them. Shop around to find someone who is used to dealing with small businesses, as they are usually less costly. In the year of writing, a payment of £275 is a reasonable fee for straightforward preparation of a tax return, and is likely to save you more than that in your tax liability. This assumes that you have kept your accounting (income and expenses) accurately and legibly during the year, and can simply hand it all over to your accountant. If you expect them to wade through messy and incomplete accounts, it will cost considerably more. After the first year, it is much easier to lessen the risk of being without the savings to pay the tax, as you will know what you paid last year, and whether your income is going up or down. This allows you to adjust what you need to put by during each year.

It is important to tell the Inland Revenue when you become self-employed. In our experience, they are generally helpful and approachable, and will be able to tell you what you need to do, including obtaining a Schedule D so that tax is not deducted at source when you invoice organizations such as training institutes with whom you may establish contracts, as it is their usual practice to do this. If you are both employed and self-employed keep separate records of your both incomes.

Thistle (1998) provides a useful guide for the tax, VAT and NI structures, which is updated by means of an insert into the book as these change.

Professional liability and indemnity

You will have set up your professional liability and indemnity scheme when you began your practice. The only risks here are not reviewing the amount involved from time to time to check that the sum insured would still cover you if a claim was made against you, and also that you keep them informed of any new venture you undertake. This ensures that everything you do is covered. Originally you might have simply stated that you are a therapist in independent employment, and later you might move on to offering occasional workshops, or ongoing training. Your indemnity does probably cover that aspect of your professional self, but it makes sense to check it out.

Capital equipment and bad debts

There are two other financial risk areas. The first is from the need to buy new capital items for your business, such as a new computer. It is prudent to keep money aside 'just in case', or invariably the old computer dies at a time when you have the least amount of available spare money. The second area is that of bad debts. These fall into two categories:

- clients whose cheques are not honoured by their banks;
- companies who take a very long time to pay your invoice.

Client debts

There is a therapeutic element to clients whose cheques 'bounce', in that clients may be attempting to tell you something they are unable to say in any other way. This could be in their conscious awareness, or out of their awareness. Perhaps there is a problem in the therapy such as the client not feeling heard or helped. There could be a change in their financial or domestic situation that they have not been able to tell you about. Assuming that the client is still working with you, it is important initially to explore possibilities that this is not simply a practical or financial matter.

In practical terms, this can sometimes be a difficult area to deal with. If you are still working with the client, you can ask them to pay you by cash to avoid further difficulties, or accept that it is a 'one-off' and hope that it will not occur again. If they are clients with whom you have finished working, then the best course of action is a polite but clear letter, explaining what has happened and asking them to reimburse you. If there is no response, and any further letters are ignored, theoretically you can take the matter to the Small Claims Court, having advised your former client that you are going to do so.

This warning letter often brings a speedy response with your money. However, if it does not, then you have to decide whether you wish to follow that route or not. This can now all be done online and in fact only goes to court if the client contests the claim.

It is not a costly business as no solicitors are involved, but it will take time to fill out the necessary paperwork and possibly to attend the hearing if it is contested. You have to weigh up your time versus the money you wish to recover. There is a very useful website about debts, how to avoid them and how to recover them at http://www.businesslink.gov.uk

As McMahon et al. (2005) comment, it is important that you have stated in your client information sheet that non-payment of fees could lead to legal action. That way, you do not have to concern yourself about issues of client confidentiality, and whether you might be breaching it.

Recently we talked with a group of independent practitioners about bad client debts, and found that in practice few of us had experienced problems. Sometimes clients forgot their chequebooks, but paid the next time. Sometimes where it seemed that it could become a problem, clients were asked to pay a session in advance. There were a couple of instances of a letter of intent to pursue the matter through the Small Claims Court, but the biggest debt and the one that was most difficult to get settled was in fact a problem with an organization, not an individual.

Slow payment of invoices

The issue of slow payment of invoices has theoretically been addressed in legislation in England and Wales that enables the independent practitioner to include a penalty clause (Bank of England base rate plus 8 per cent) where companies do not pay within the specified and agreed term. This does not mean that you will always get paid on time, sadly. Often it is not the person with whom you have contracted who is responsible for paying your invoice. They probably simply sign it off and send it to the finance department, and it is here that the problems can arise. It can take enormous amounts of time wasted on the telephone or writing letters before you receive your deserved payment.

It will help if you have correctly included any contract reference numbers on your original invoice, by whom it was commissioned and clear details of what service you provided. Some delays are purely and simply down to the fact that finance offices do not know which particular departmental account to assign your invoice to, and rather than them contacting you to find out more, your invoice lands in a pending folder. Being accurate with your invoices can save you time and ensure prompt payment.

Whether it is worth a decision to press the penalty clause or not is something only you can judge. On the one hand, it often does bring about results. On the other, you may fear upsetting your contact and thereby risking losing any further work from them. It is usually worth talking to them, explaining the problem, and asking if they can expedite matters for you, before taking any other action. Often they feel embarrassed that you have been kept waiting and will do everything they can to clear up the matter.

One other way of helping to avoid slow payments is to offer a reduced fee for prompt payment. This reduction could in fact be your usual fee, and therefore your 'full fee' has already built in an extra payment for late payment. It can work very well, though it does not solve every delay.

As in the case of individual client non-payment matters, you can resort to the Small Claims Court, provided your claim is for under £5000. Once again, the stated intention of doing so does often bring results. Having said all of the above, bad debts are in reality not often a major issue in independent practice.

SAFETY RISKS

There are various elements to safety:

- your own safety;
- clients' safety;
- the safety of others.

Personal safety

When working on your own, very often you do not have the built-in personal safety elements of working within an organization. As Field (2007) says, this is particularly relevant if we are working from home or indeed in rented premises with no one else on site. When we assess people, since we do not know who they are, their history or their issue, personal safety should be considered. If it is possible, having someone else around unobtrusively is a wise precaution. If this is an impossibility in practice, then try to make it seem as if there is someone else there. The sound of a radio, or of a washing machine going, which can be heard as you answer the door, though not in your practice room, may give a subliminal message that you are not alone.

You may decide that you will not work with a client who has a history of violence, though of course they may choose to hide this in an initial assessment, even if you have asked the question. If you do work with them, think carefully about how you will protect yourself if necessary. If you have not thought this through beforehand, you both risk your own safety and may find that the issue is somehow present in the room and disrupts the therapeutic alliance. Some independent practitioners choose to have either a panic button or a squawking hand-held personal alarm near them. If this helps to ensure safety, then buy one. Other practitioners believe that the mere presence of such a device, even if the client is unaware of it, will interfere with building up trust, and so reject using alarms.

Other sensible measures include an entrance that is well lit and a room that allows an easy exit (for you as well as the client). Think where your room is actually situated. A room on ground floor level is generally safer than one on an upper floor, both in the practical aspect of you leaving the premises if necessary, and also psychologically because it appears to be more part of the reception area of premises.

Though it is absolutely necessary to think through personal safety measures, it is very rare that they do come into play in our work. If, once you have reflected on the matter, you are still uneasy, then think about sharing premises with another practitioner and agree about the hours that you will both work in your individual rooms there. You may also to have to accept that while you may be very skilled and experienced in dealing with some clients in an organizational setting, they are not clients or client issues you choose to work with independently.

In talking with the same group of independent practitioners mentioned above, we heard some interesting and concerning tales about when people had felt threatened, from someone exposing himself, to someone saying they had a gun with them. However, what became extremely clear was that these occurrences were in fact very rare, and that if sensible precautions are taken, we are probably no more at risk than if working in an organization. However, those precautions do need to be taken.

Client safety

There is then the issue of client safety. Again there are two elements here. The first is their safety from injury while on your premises, and for that you need to have your insurance and indemnity policies in place. If they trip on a loose carpet, or on an uneven paving stone, you could be facing a compensation claim.

The second element concerns the client's psychological safety, and whether they are likely to cause harm to themselves. Bond and Mitchels (2008), when considering what action therapists might take, suggest we consider:

■ real risk;
■ serious harm;
■ imminent harm;
■ effective action.

If the lack of safety is imminent, for example, we might take action, including breaking confidentiality that we would not take if the risk was more distant, and we had time to consult our supervisor or other professional colleagues.

Suicide

One of the obvious concerns for client safety is that of risk of suicide. It poses one of the most difficult dilemmas for independent practitioners, who feel alone and without the resources of an organization to draw on. It is important to think clearly and not be carried away by thoughts of 'what if' about our business, but also to stay focused on this client.

Even if you are happy with your belief that it is everyone's right to end their life if they choose to do so, you need to be aware that the client's relatives may hold a different view. And it is still illegal to do so or assist someone with this in the UK. Once again this is where you need to have drawn up a clear contract with your client, which indicates whether confidentiality includes occasions when you believe that he may harm himself. This could include things other than suicide, such as extensive cutting, abusing drugs or alcohol etc. If you have not done this, then whatever action you take could be seen as not putting the client's interest first. 'Dammed if you do, and dammed if you don't.'

Breaking confidentiality

Before you do anything, consider the legal aspects of that action – the therapeutic consequences are dealt with elsewhere in the book. Contact with the client's GP may seem the obvious thing to do, but have you made it clear beforehand that in cases of harm to self, you would make that contact? If not, and the GP inserts 'suicidal ideation', 'suicide attempt' or 'serious self-harming behaviour' into the client's medical notes, which later means that the client is refused health insurance, or turned down for a job they might have otherwise expected to get, you potentially could be sued by the client for breach of confidentiality. You would need to be very sure that you could defend yourself on the grounds of suspecting mental illness, or risk to others through the client's self-harming actions. Such claims could be very costly, both financially and also to your reputation if there is press coverage. This could happen even if the judgement is in your favour.

Another risk area, apart from any legal implications of breaking confidentiality in terms of self-harm, is how far you wish to extend your involvement with the client. This may sound harsh and unempathetic at first glance. In reality, there are practical risks for you. You may not have the spare capacity, in terms of client spaces, or emotional capacity at that time, to offer the support the client needs. Are you able to provide extra sessions and do your personal circumstances allow you to take telephone calls from this client at frequent intervals during a crisis? Do not promise what you cannot sensibly fulfil.

Strategies for dealing with client safety

In order for you to deal with the risk, you can think ahead and put various strategies into place. You could:

- keep one slot per day for emergency appointments;
- prepare a list of useful help lines, such as the Samaritans (telephone, text and online information), self harm, addiction and abuse organizations;
- ensure that you have your own backup such as supervision, psychiatric support, medical advice etc.;
- keep up to date with professional thinking;
- know how you can help the client to access other support such as a psychiatric referral, crisis team etc.;
- be prepared to suggest that the client sees his GP, and possibly offer also to talk to the GP yourself, if this does not contradict your beliefs about client autonomy;
- be prepared to make an onward referral if you are not able to give the necessary commitment yourself – this implies having already researched local possibilities in preparation for such a need;
- challenge your own thinking if you have a tendency to fall into the 'I must be able to provide everything for my clients' position;
- above all, be able to discuss possibilities openly and clearly with your clients, both in general terms during intake and assessment procedures, and more specifically as the need arises.

Client harm to others

The last area of risk to safety is that of harm to others by the client. Again you have covered this with your client when you contracted with them, but that does not stop it becoming a dilemma sometimes. Just what is the risk to another? Is your client telling you what he intends to do, or revealing something at a psychological level, which does not pose a real threat to anyone else? If the client demands your assurance of confidentiality over some action, remember that they are consciously or unconsciously manipulating you into respecting their needs more than those of another person.

Bond and Mitchels (2008) reflect that the law is clearer on what constitutes the need to take action than we are sometimes about our personal and professional integrity. Many of us glibly reel off the limits of confidentiality when contracting, citing terrorism, the Children Act etc., but do not really expect to have to make many disclosures resulting from what our adult clients may tell us. (If you work with young people, then the Children Act is much more likely to have significance in your daily life.) Bond and Mitchel's book provides an extremely useful chart showing where there is a therapist's duty under the law to take action.

Even this outline does leave the independent practitioner having to make serious judgements. There are areas where it depends on the balance of public interest. Take the case of your client inflicting physical harm on another adult. Common law requires the prevention of serious physical harm – but what is serious? There is a grey area surrounding psychological harm, especially if it involves another vulnerable adult.

In the rare case of a client disclosing that he has in the past, or still is, abusing a child, it is likely that the therapist may have to take some action. If there is no current abuse, then it may be therapeutically more useful to work with the client to make their own disclosures as appropriate. However, if the abuse is current, then the therapist is likely to be in a position of needing to break confidentiality. While bearing in mind that the client has been made aware of this at the contracting stage, and may be disclosing as a way of getting further help, it is vital that the therapist is not catapulted into hasty action without thinking through how to breach confidentiality. Again supervision and access to legal help is vital. The obvious place to break confidentiality is with social services, and what stops us doing so is a fear that the system will let the young person down, as we have heard in many well publicized cases. Will they be left in danger, or at even greater risk, because the abuser is well aware that this has been reported and nothing has been done.

We would recommend that you set up an arrangement that enables you to access legal support when you need it, that you read books dealing with safety of clients and legal responsibilities, such as Bond and Mitchel's and that you keep up to date through CPD and your professional journals with what is required of you, and what is good practice.

Another important aspect is good supervision and peer support.

> **Harriet**: I find it really difficult thinking about all the things that could go wrong. I tend to bury my head a bit, I suppose.
>
> **Norman**: I'm a bit the same, but talking this through today has made me realize that that's probably not the best option.
>
> **Belinda**: I need to find a workshop on suicide and what my position is around confidentiality.
>
> ⮕

Norman: Yes, and I also want to read a lot more about legal responsibilities. I've bought the book you mentioned, but it sits on my bookshelf to be read 'at some point'. It's probably already out of date!

LEGAL ISSUES

The final area of risk we will look at here is that of being asked for information by a solicitor, having to appear as a witness in a court case, and action taken against you as a therapist. Often these areas raise huge anxieties in the minds of independent practitioners, although in reality, most of us do not often find ourselves in such a position. The issues are raised here, but we would urge you to read specialized writings dealing more fully with such situations and to consult your professional body if you find yourself needing advice and support.

Requests for information about clients

For therapists, the most usual requests for information about past or present clients come from solicitors who are acting either for the client or for someone taking action against them. They may simply ask if Joe Bloggs has been your client, or may ask for more specific information about the counselling process and its outcomes. In all cases, before doing anything else, consult your client to ask them if they will allow you to disclose any information. If you do not do so, then you may be in breach of the general duty of confidentiality. If they agree to this, ask for this to be put into writing, with any agreed limitations to what you may disclose. In practice, it can often be sensible to share anything that you may write hereafter to the requesting solicitor, so that you do have their informed consent. This may slow the process down, but does ensure that the client is fully aware of what has been said.

If they do not agree to you giving any information, then you are not obliged to do so. However, in some cases, you could be subject to a court order to disclose confidences. This can be done by means of a subpoena, requiring the therapist to attend a court at a certain time with their notes as set out in the summons, where it will be decided whether or not the documents are relevant to the matter. The other way is by an application to the High Court for a disclosure of the notes. Neither of these actions necessarily results in the notes actually being disclosed. That will depend on whether it is thought they are relevant and necessary at that time to the case. Whatever transpires, this can be an anxious time for therapists, particularly those in independent practice, without the backup of an organization. If you are in this position, it is essential to make sure that you do seek the help and support of supervisors and other professionals.

Witness

If you find yourself in the position of appearing as a witness, like most people, you may find it challenging and possibly terrifying. You may also be asked to be a expert witness in a case where you have had no previous involvement. For example, one of the authors undertakes this role in cases dealing with child custody, medical negligence and airline practices. It may be easier if you have already submitted a clear and comprehensive report, because then you are able to refer to it in court. The other thing to bear in mind is that unlike most TV dramas, it is not common practice to abusively attack you, even when your expertise is being challenged. Do not be afraid to ask for time to reflect on a question before answering, or to say that there is not a 'right' answer if this is indeed the case.

Client complaint

Possibly the worst case scenario for any therapist is for a client to bring a complaint or a legal action against them. Even if the complaint is not upheld, it can be an extremely stressful and sometimes long drawn out period to live through. Ensure that you have the necessary documentation, such as your notes, for as long a period as a complaint can be made – usually up to six years. This gives more credibility to any statement that you make, since you are not simply relying on your memory.

Find out as much about the process as possible beforehand, so that you can prepare yourself fully. It is quite reasonable to ask about this, and the information should be forthcoming. As has been emphasized above, seek support from your own profession and any other professionals, such as solicitors. In many complaints procedures, you are entitled to have a support person alongside you. They may not be able to speak, but their presence may help you to feel more grounded, and they can also take notes for you, as it is often difficult to remember things when you are under pressure.

CONCLUSION

We hope that reading this chapter has not dismayed you. There are risks inherent in independent practice, but the vast majority of therapists emerge unscathed at the end of a satisfying career. The best way to practise safely is to be aware of the risks, and take steps to minimize them.

Reflexive Points

- Take time to read around the subjects of confidentiality and legal issues in therapeutic work. Use up-to-date sources, as the law does change.
- Use a supervision session to discuss issues concerning harm to both self and others by clients, and what you steps you might take under what circumstances. While this can only be theoretical, it could be useful in the future to have done this preliminary thinking.
- Reflect on your workplace, whether at home or in rented premises. Look at it with an outsider's eye and consider any safety aspects that need review or action.
- Carry out a risk assessment of your practice. Once you have done this, note down action points. Review this assessment at regular intervals.

Chapter 10

Managing Risk: Crunch Factors for Your Business

INTRODUCTION

It may seem a bit pessimistic of us to include a chapter on 'crunch factors' – we do not wish to alarm readers or dwell too much on the negatives and hypothetical 'what ifs'. However, as two experienced mentors of colleagues working in private practice, we recognize the risks to one's livelihood and reputation of independent practice and these cannot be ignored. We asked some of our colleagues who have recently begun to work independently whether this chapter should be included and this comment sums up their reactions: 'If only I had known about some of the pitfalls, I might have saved myself a lot of heartache!' We are offering some ideas and insights into business failure generally, and specifically why independent therapy practices either never get off the ground or simply falter at key stages. No doubt there will be areas that we have missed, and some that do not seem immediately relevant for your particular situation.

Starting out in independent practice carries with it significant challenges and particular risks. We touched on some of the reasons for people choosing this way of working in Chapter 1, but therapists typically choose to work in independent practice because there may be demand or referrals that require us to respond to a client's need in this context. In this sense, it may be unforeseen but become a welcome addition to your portfolio of work.

The Case Study of Alex's Experience

He had been working in a young people's organization that offers short-term counselling for 11–25 year olds. A colleague in the same organization had been unsuccessfully seeking a counsellor to refer a client on, as more work was wanted by the client and was felt to be beneficial. The parents were able and prepared to pay. Eventually she asked Alex if he would see the client privately. This involved a great deal of discussion in Alex's supervision and with his line manager as to the ethics of taking a referral from one of the agency's clients. It was decided that as there appeared to be no other counsellor in the area who was prepared to work with a 14-year-old, it was in the client's best interests. After working with this client, Alex found that other referrals followed – these were nothing to do with the agency in which he worked. Then adults began to enquire, and Alex's private practice was growing. After about a year, he decided to reduce his work in the agency to three days a week, and spend the other two on his independent work.

A further incentive to starting in independent practice may be knowing another colleague who is doing it and feeling inspired by their success and enjoyment of this activity. Mary had kept in touch with her fellow students from her training some years previously, and realized that a number had moved into independent practice. When talking to them, she felt that she too would like to try this.

Of course, we may also enter into independent practice because it may be of necessity, as we mentioned at the beginning of the book. Self-employment may be the main or only means to practise our skills in a location where there may be health service based counsellors and therapists but no options for people who would like to consult with an independent practitioner, or where there is a waiting list for NHS counsellors.

The intentions and motivation that the examples above demonstrate may bear little relation to success when working in independent practice, although happily these particular practitioners have been successful.

As we mentioned in the introduction, few, if any, therapists have been trained in setting up, developing and running a practice or business. None of the practitioners we discussed this with had had any input on their main professional training courses. Indeed, we have come across very few courses in counselling, psychotherapy or clinical or counselling psychology that specifically teach skills for developing an independent practice. There are occasionally workshops advertised, which typically cover this topic in a single day at most. Most of us have had to rely on our intuition as well as on trial and error experience in order to develop skills in this area. A fortunate few have had transferable skills from previous careers.

Simply offering psychological therapy is on its own is insufficient under-pinning to running an independent practice. In the role of independent practitioner in therapy, we quickly learn to be our own secretary, accounts clerk, cash flow manager, marketing and sales executive, maybe even office cleaner, coffee maker, IT specialist and debt collector! In addition, we have to find time for our own continuing professional development, business planning, doing our accounts, visiting the bank and maintaining our premises or consulting room.

One of our colleagues told us that if she had realized all that was involved before she started, perhaps she would have never taken the plunge. She had solely imagined herself sitting in her newly designed, very beautiful room with her clients. On the other hand, she also said that it would have been useful to know more, as she had not initially allowed enough time for these activities and had found it hard to balance her time. Perhaps the ideal is to maintain awareness that you will not simply be in that beautiful room, but not to be overwhelmed by the other activities that might kill your passion for your work.

Few of us when we start out are in a position in which to hire others, such as a PA or secretary, to help with some of these functions. Most of us never choose or need to employ others. If we neglect any of the tasks, however, we run a risk of experiencing difficulties, or even worse, encoun-tering failure in our independent practice. We are arguably at our most vulnerable commercially and clinically when starting out in independent practice, or at least in our first year or two. This is when we have to acquire and hone many new and possibly unfamiliar skills.

> John's summary is enlightening. 'I had to maintain a focus on developing my practice, marketing it and adapting my approach to therapy to what clients were seeking. It was also the time when my expenses were at their highest as I needed to purchase new equipment and enter into a lease agreement for consulting rooms. This all happened when my cash flow wasn't yet guaran-teed or in a steady state. The bank that has loaned me money was watching closely how my business was developing. At times my personal confidence in running a business was at zero. I almost forgot to mention that I still wanted to find time for my personal life, social relationships, domestic chores and the like! And on top of all of this, time (and money) for continuing profes-sional development and clinical supervision had to be found. I feel sorry for people starting now when the recession may be biting.'

Another reason for businesses failing is that when your practice is up and running in a steady state and reasonably successful and you receive an increasing number of new referrals, you may be less inclined to put your mind to some of the more mundane aspects of running your business. However, you cannot take things for granted and continued success requires ongoing planning, marketing and, of course, sound and effective clinical practice.

Developing a bad reputation for how you manage your business affairs could negatively affect your clinical practice, and vice versa. When times are good in terms of client flow, our personal shortcomings and lack of business acumen may be less noticeable and relevant. However, you should not lose sight of the challenges, which, like unconscious processes, are always present but may only reveal themselves at times of difficulty or crisis, thereby making the job of running a business even more difficult. Apply what we know through our psychological training to our business management.

It is a reasonable supposition that nobody starts out in independent practice seeking to fail. However, for a number of different reasons, this outcome may become inevitable if specific challenges that present are not adequately and successfully dealt with, so below we offer some pointers to avoid this.

BUSINESS MENTOR

In the same way that every qualified practitioner is required to have regular supervision for their clinical work, it is good practice for any counsellor or therapist working independently to have access to a business mentor and/or supervisor or trusted colleague. This is someone who can help you to reflect on your progress in developing your business, as well as share their skills and experience. The skills of a clinical supervisor may differ from those of a business mentor. It is not always the case that your clinical supervisor will be doubly skilled in running an independent counselling or psychotherapy practice. For this reason, it may be necessary to be supervised by or seek consultation with two different professionals, each of whom is able to address the two disparate needs of clinical supervision and practice management that we may have as practitioners working in independent practice.

Let John speak again.

I think that some independent practices fail because the practitioner, while having good intentions and being strongly motivated, doesn't have the specific business skills in growing their practice, cash flow management and establishing a network for referrals, to name but a few requirements for success. The danger of neglecting business mentorship is more acute when we feel overwhelmed with clinical work. That may be good news in terms of client flow but oddly doesn't necessarily lead to positive financial success. Mentorship is also ironically needed the most when the rate of flow of our new referrals has all but dried up, but at that time, we are afraid to invest time, money and effort into seeking a business mentor for our practice because we worry about the financial implications of this undertaking. So it's useful for both the peaks and troughs of our journey.

But just as we help our clients to deepen or to better understand their feelings and behaviour during times of personal crisis and to respond to life's difficulties in more adaptive ways to help them gain insight and overcome them, so we as independent practitioners are challenged by our mentors to better understand our challenges, to adapt to changing circumstances, acquire new skills and to hone our clinical practice. At least that is my experience. It's odd really: if we were helping our clients to find their way forward, we would know all this. But sometimes we don't apply it to ourselves.

THE MAIN REASONS WHY INDEPENDENT PRACTICES FAIL

Every therapist working as an independent practitioner is likely to experience some similar challenges to every other practitioner, as well as a number that will be unique to themselves. For example, all practitioners will need to think about referral sources and the premises where they will see their clients. In this sense, these are challenges in common.

The unique issues, however, may be to do with setting fees, how you will manage your finances, when you see clients, what sort of problems you treat and what competition you may face. It is important to try to identify and understand as many of these challenges as possible before setting out in independent practice. Identifying a number of these challenges does not mean that you should not set up in or develop your own independent practice. Instead, listing the challenges can help you to hone your ideas, challenge you to think what may make your practice distinct or niche, and enable you to focus more intensely on your unique skills as well as on your clinical and commercial talents.

Those readers who have watched the television series *The Apprentice* will be familiar with the idea that one need not be an expert in a particular area of business or enterprise in order to succeed. However, that programme also highlights the common deficiencies of prospective entrepreneurs and many of the lessons apply to those of us who work in independent practice. Below, we briefly describe a number of reasons for independent practices failing. Although we have tried to put these in order of importance, evidence suggests that failure to attend to any one of these could jeopardize a business. While some may be more commonly presenting challenges, it may give false reassurance if we simply attend to those that may seem more likely to occur.

No local need

Your intentions may be good in that you feel that people in your local area would benefit from having the option of seeing a therapist privately. However, there may simply be no need for this. For this reason, your practice may never get off the ground or you may have a false start insofar as you receive occasional referrals but never enough for the practice to be properly launched and to reach a steady state in terms of referrals. Simply 'setting up shop', just as Lucy does in the *Peanuts* cartoon strip, and declaring that 'the Doctor is IN' is no guarantee that clients will need or seek such a service. In smaller communities, this may be even more the case as people may worry that their seeking therapy will become common knowledge among others in the area, so they specifically avoid the local independent therapist.

Nothing that makes you stand out from the crowd

Reputation is core to the whole success of your practice. But you also need to stand out from other colleagues in some unique and positive ways that highlight and define your particular skills and attributes. We are not suggesting that you must be better than other practitioners, but in a highly competitive independent practice market, and in an increasingly cost conscious one, clients need to feel some special affinity and motivation to come to meet you as opposed to your competition. So just as we sometimes begin a therapeutic session by asking clients 'Why now?' so we need to ask ourselves 'Why me?' when thinking what might attract clients.

Lack of initial finance

Inadequate funding or trying to develop your practice 'on the cheap' could be detrimental to its success. You may need to put money into your business before it even gets off the ground or any profits are realized. This is the reason why we explored business plans in Chapter 5. Failure to keep overhead costs low is a major cause of business failure.

Avoiding marketing

We looked at marketing in depth in Chapter 8. It is sufficient here to remind ourselves that a lack of marketing can impede progress in setting up and running independent practices. While a steady flow of referrals from a colleague may be welcome and help to reassure you that you are on the right track, things can change. It may be that you are no longer 'flavour of the month' with your colleagues or there may be new competition where you practise. It is important to keep looking beyond where things stand and always to prepare for an uncertain future. At worst good marketing can help to maintain a healthy practice and at best it can ensure its steady growth over a number of years.

Not keeping up to date professionally

Failure to see where things are going in psychological therapy generally can result in your skills and therapeutic approach becoming obsolete to the needs of your clients. While this statement might raise a few hackles, as we do not wish to become people who change our approach in the same way as we might change our coat, we do need to recognize that client-centredness is about responding in a way that is clinically relevant to the needs of your clients. Clients and referrers may seek specific therapeutic styles or skills.

One example is the rising interest and awareness among potential clients of cognitive behaviour therapy. While many therapists are not 'wedded' to CBT as the only modality within which they practise, we must recognize that clients increasingly ask therapists for specific 'brands' of therapy based on their knowledge and experience, having accessed the Internet or been recommended to them by a friend or GP. Acquiring skills in other therapeutic approaches can help you to remain relevant to prospective clients. This can also extend to having therapeutic skills that enable you to work more briefly, which may be especially relevant for clients who may not have the financial resources for medium- or longer-term therapy.

Being seen as a specialist

While there are advantages in having a specialism that makes you stand out from the crowd, as we said above, there are also risks. If you practise within a narrow framework, you increase the risk of putting all your eggs in one basket.

Take Emma, for example, who defined herself as a specialist in working with clients affected by post-traumatic stress disorder. She built up a good reputation in this specialism, and for a while provided training courses for other practitioners over a wide geographical area, as well as having referrals from outside her immediate vicinity. For various reasons, this work slowed down, and Emma gradually found that she had much less work. In her local area, being seen as a PTSD specialist, more general clients were not being referred to her, so she had to return to some basic marketing to build up a wider portfolio again. As she said, she needed to highlight her other competencies to potential referrers so that they knew that she was not just a 'one trick pony'.

No business plan

If you do not have a well structured business plan, you have no reference point or way to map your progress as your practice develops. You need a guide as to where you are heading, as well as a measure of whether you have attained the targets that you have set. To quote the old saying: 'a man (or a woman) going nowhere usually gets there' again. If nowhere is where you want to be, then ignore business planning! There is detailed information about business plans in Chapter 5.

It does not indicate failure, however, if you do not attain these targets, but at least you will know if you are off track sooner rather than later. Then you can adjust your management or clinical skills in order to bring yourself back on track or change direction if that is what is called for. If you are planning to borrow money from a bank in order to set up in independent practice, you will almost inevitably be required to present a business plan.

Unexpected events

Catastrophic failure in life and business is rare, but it can happen to any one of us. Unanticipated or unforeseen events can seriously interfere with our ability to run or manage our practice. In some, cases it can prevent us from practising altogether. An extreme example is an accusation of professional misconduct, which could mean that while under investigation your time and energies are severely curtailed. Even though a significant proportion of accusations are not proven, effort, stress and overall distraction from your business could prove crippling.

Sadly, further disasters can occur in our personal life. These could include personal loss such as that of a loved one, the onset of health problems or even litigation in our work arena, all of which could detract from our ability to practise.

Ignoring changes in regulation

Changes in regulations that govern how we practise do not cause our practice to fail by themselves, but they can interfere with our ability to succeed. For example, the professional regulation of counsellors and psychotherapists is undertaken by the British Association for Counselling and Psychotherapy as well as the United Kingdom Council for Psychotherapy. Psychologists' professional registration has been transferred to the Health Professions Council and, at the time of writing, it is likely that counsellors and psychotherapists will also do so. If practitioners ignore these changes, they could find themselves in the position of being unable to practise. So it is essential to keep abreast of and prepare for changes on the horizon.

Taking your eye off the big picture

There is a risk for any practitioner that you may get bogged down with or fixated with particular areas of practice but fail to mind your whole business. An example is the dispute that Felicity had with a client over the late payment of a bill. It was a large amount so it was reasonable that it took her attention, but as she admitted, she became fixated with this. It meant that she was less energetic and creative as a practitioner for her other clients, and found that a number dropped out of therapy before completing the work. Luckily she realized what was happening before it was too late to reverse the trend.

You may also have less time available for other important aspects of business if you have a heavy clinical case load. There are classic examples from business management and administration where large enterprises and multinational firms have failed as a result of seemingly small issues bogging down the entire organization. The same can apply to the independent practitioner and the risk is arguably greater as there is often no one who can take over functions in order to maintain other aspects of the business while a specific matter is addressed.

While it may sound tedious and unexciting, you do need to monitor overall progress of the business frequently. It may be insufficient, for example, to provide superb psychological therapy but at the same time be unable to maintain a close eye on your bank balance, having underdeveloped IT skills or poor record keeping, all of which may cause distress to the practitioner.

Even in a one-person business, cash flow is essential and those who work in independent practice as therapists are no exception to this rule. If your debts are high, you become bogged down with cash flow problems, you get behind in your billing or accounts pile up, you may eventually be out of business, no matter how good your work with clients has been.

Forgetting natural cycles in income

Failure to plan for normal variation in client numbers can also threaten your livelihood. There will be times in the year when new client flow may reduce or indeed disappear altogether, while existing clients may think about terminating therapy. This could be during extended summer holidays, over Easter and Christmas or indeed at other times that may be more apparent as you gain knowledge of your local area. While these cycles may be normal, you need to plan for these variations or you may find yourself being out of pocket. It may be preferable to plan for your own holidays when most of your clients are likely to take theirs.

The following conversation took place during a meeting of three independent practitioners.

Maddie: How are you guys finding client numbers at the moment?

Brent: Mine are right down at present, which is why I booked my holiday for this month.

Maddie: So where are you off to? Was that a last minute deal?

Brent: I'm off to Spain for a fortnight. No, I booked it ages ago.

Maddie: Lucky for you it coincided with this drop in clients then!

Jeannie: Brent always takes his main holiday this month, Maddie.

Maddie: How come?

Brent: Just think, Maddie – what is happening in this place during this month?

Maddie: Can't think of anything special.　　　　　　　　　　▮▶

Jeannie: The processing plant shuts down for two weeks for maintenance.

Maddie: Yes, but that's not where all the clients come from.

Jeannie: No, but if you think about it, loads of the employees from there go on holiday during this period. The shops are dead as a result, so some of their employees take holidays too, and the school has introduced a two-week half term break, so parents can take children away without problems now. It all makes a difference.

Oversupply of therapists

There may be saturation in your local therapy market. However good a therapist you may be, there may still be others who are better known locally or who have already established a practice. Check this out before you start! You could do this by looking in the local Yellow Pages, consulting professional directories and doing online searches. It is also worth asking professional friends and colleagues in independent practice about the current state of the local market.

The wrong fee structure

You may price yourself out of the market. This can work in both directions. It is obvious that if your fee is too high, clients will not be able to afford many sessions, if any, with you. Equally, however, if you underprice yourself, prospective clients may baulk at the idea of coming to you as they may question your competency, particularly if others in the local area charge significantly more. Once again, you can check current fees through professional directories such as that of the BACP, or ring the therapists in your area to check what they are charging. If you are too embarrassed to do this, get a non-therapist friend to do it for you.

Being a 'Jack of all trades'

When we began our independent practice, like most people we did everything, from all the paperwork necessary for our accounts to the cleaning. We could not afford to do anything else, as paying someone else would have eaten into our profits in this early stage – in fact probably reduced them to zero.

However, once you are established, you might ask yourself if you are getting bogged down in what you are not very good at. Could anything be outsourced in order to leave us free to do the things we are best at? If, for example, you are not a very fast typist and you are not a well organized bookkeeper, you might employ someone to do your typing and book-keeping. There are online secretarial services where you can outsource these needs at significantly less cost to you than employing somebody on your own premises. Having a good accountant is also valuable unless you fully understand how best to manage your finances and what expenses you can reasonably claim. However, be warned: sensible as this may be in the long run, spending too much on these areas of your business in its early days could wipe out any profit.

Your own traits

From a psychological perspective, there are certain traits that may militate against success in independent practice. These include being overly confident and ignoring the risks of having no business plan. A further one is just a sense that you will succeed on the back of your reputation, without putting in any real effort to your marketing. So how well do you really know yourself, and will you take this into account or ignore it? There are various personality questionnaires that you could use to check out the likelihood of success. These include the Honey and Mumford Learning Styles Questionnaire and the Myers–Briggs Type Inventory. While completing these in their original forms is expensive and requires you to engage with someone who has the necessary training to administer them, you can find versions that provide a rough guide free on the Internet.

Alternatively, you could try this reflective exercise:

First prepare a list or a mind map of all the parts of running an independent prac-tice. Then use a favourite relaxation exercise to clear your mind of distractions.

Now let your mind wander over the various aspects of working in independent practice. These could include not going to an organization every day, or waiting for clients to contact you. Imagine sitting doing the paperwork and invoices, and finding ways of attracting work. Visualize your practice room and working with clients there.

Give time to all the things you wrote on your list or mind map. As you do this exercise, keep in your awareness your physical and emotional responses to each area.

⟶

When you have finished this reflection, jot down your recollections, and use these to list what you will be good at and what may cause you problems. By yourself or with a friend, look at whether these recollections and reactions related to your more general personality traits, and whether there is anything that could cause you serious concern in beginning your business.

Forgetting to listen to your client

One of the greatest risks in working in independent practice (indeed in salaried practice as well) is not listening to your client. This may seem obvious in a book that is aimed at therapists, whose primary role it is to listen to their client! However, when clients are paying for their sessions, their expectations may be higher. Given the expense to them, if clients feel that their problems are not being solved, their needs are not being met and there is a lack of congruence and empathy between themselves and their therapist, the relationship will quickly end. We need to tune into both therapeutically and also with our business ear to the client at times. Therefore it makes sense to ask a version of this question at frequent intervals – we tend to use it at the end of each session – 'Has this session been helpful to you today? Is there anything we need to change in the way we work to make it more useful to you?'

MINIMIZING RISKS

We have highlighted above some of the most common reasons why independent counselling and psychotherapy practices fail. None is necessarily more important than the other since each person's circumstances are different. There are, however, a number of positive steps that you can take as practitioners in order to reduce the risk of difficulties or failure in your practice.

Forming networks

It may help to join a community of like-minded people. If there are other private practitioners local to you, rather than viewing them as competitors, there may be certain benefits to forming a close working relationship with them. The reason for this is that other colleagues may, through their generosity, share ideas, hints and tips for how to deal with local conditions relating to marketing, premises and the like, which could be of enormous mutual benefit. Secondly, if you are away, on leave or indisposed and unable to practise, one of your colleagues may act as a locum or at least be willing to take up referrals in your absence. Furthermore, other colleagues may come to recognize your unique skills and expertise and therefore refer clients whom they feel less confident to work with. Their support and awareness of your own practice could prove invaluable.

If you are thinking about starting in independent practice and do not yet know other practitioners in your area, you could ask your supervisor if he or she knows anyone else in your position. We have worked with groups of supervisees who are all in the first stages of setting up their practice, and this has enabled a very fruitful sharing of ideas, resources and support. After a while working with us, we have suggested that they might want to self-facilitate, and this has also proved very successful for them – as well as being a cheaper option!

Staying passionate

It is important that you enjoy what you are doing. This may seem obvious but in any business there will be difficult and trying times. If you stop enjoying what you are doing, you are less likely to practise creatively and effectively. This could also come to damage your reputation. If you stop enjoying the challenge of running a business, reflect on what you can do to rekindle your passion. If you cannot, it may be time to think about salaried employment, a sabbatical or taking up another profession altogether.

Becoming a specialist

While we have highlighted the risks of developing expertise in a specialist area of psychological therapy, it can also afford you several other benefits. You are more likely to be approached by the media for interviews, which could be helpful in terms of your marketing. Prospective clients may also seek you out above other therapists because of your reputation. Their positive experience of being helped by you could then be extended within their own social networks and they may recommend you to friends and family.

CONCLUSION

Remember that success in independent practice may not be directly linked to your motivation, although this is obviously a necessary precondition.

Businesses fail for many different reasons but this may be avoidable in some situations. 'Independent' does not necessarily mean practising alone. You can discuss your ideas and plans with colleagues, your supervisor or a practice mentor. Developing a professional support system for you may be one of the best decisions you make because you can benefit from the advice and guidance of others as you go about developing your independent practice. Before moving on to the next chapter, which looks at running your practice, you might like to reflect on some of the questions below.

Reflexive Points

- Do you consider that a business mentor is necessary to help you with your independent practice? List the pros and cons from your perspective. If you decide that it might be a worthwhile step, how might you find one? What contacts do you have already?
- Re-read the headings of the reasons why independent practices fail. Are there any that might apply more to you than others? If so, do you have ideas about avoiding the pitfalls?
- You might go through the headings again with someone who knows you well, and see if they agree.

Chapter 11

Running the Practice and Support Networks

INTRODUCTION

There are a number of areas that will help you develop and run your practice. Some of them focus on external contacts and others are more to do with assessing your personal or internal needs. In the first throes of setting up the business, it is easy to concentrate on the external factors, but in doing so, you may lose sight of your reasons for deciding to become an independent practitioner. The result can be that you become disillusioned or dissatisfied with your work. We have mentioned many of these areas in earlier chapters, but here we will examine them in more depth. If you have been in independent practice for a while, you may find, as we did, that reviewing these areas helps to revitalize your work, and re-establish good practice.

You need to consider what will make the difference here between success and failure, including overstretching yourself. Have you realistically thought through the reasons previously mentioned about why businesses fail, such as:

- Is your idea of what you want to do realistic and will bring in sufficient income?
- Do you already have good contacts? If not, do you have ideas about how to make them?
- Are you in a good enough state of health to begin?
- Have you thought about how to manage the downsides of being independent?
- Are you resilient enough to cope with the inevitable times of disappointment when things do not go to plan?

EXTERNAL CONTACTS

Let's start with the external contacts that you need to sustain your successful business. Most successful independent practitioners do not depend solely on self-referrers, but also actively seek to make contact with other professionals who may send them clients. These include GPs, employee assistance programmes, social services, schools etc.

GPs

Although increasingly GPs either have counsellors attached to their practices or refer patients through NHS systems, there are often fairly long waiting lists, and the number of sessions available may well be limited. It is therefore worth your while making contacts with GPs so that they are aware of your existence and might pass your details to patients, or at least be prepared to have your leaflets in the waiting area of their surgeries.

GPs are usually under time pressures, and so, first, you need to have clearly thought through your approach to them. It is essential to appear businesslike and professional in the way you present both yourself and your material (business cards, leaflets etc.). Remember this is a part of marketing yourself and your service.

What is it you are hoping for from the GP? Do you want patients to be given your details or do you simply want to make the GP aware that you exist? If it is the latter, then you may find that unless you take some positive steps, you will move quickly out of mind. So determinedly, though politely, leave some information – perhaps your business card and a one-page sheet of information about yourself and your service, or obtain permission to leave your leaflet for clients in the reception area. If you offer CBT, currently that would probably catch the GP's interest.

If you are fortunate, the GP may be interested in talking to you about exactly what you can offer, so be ready to be clear and specific. If there are certain groups of patients who would suit your way of working, say so. If you have a specialism, such as working with addictions, depression or couples, make sure you get that in. Lastly, although you may feel loath to do so, say what you cannot or will not work with. It is better to do this now, rather than have referrals that you have to say you cannot work with, and risk appearing to be turning away work when it is offered.

The GP may be used to dealing with sales representatives from drug companies making all sorts of claims about their products, and therefore rightly will ask you searching questions about your qualifications, experience and the way you work. This is an opportunity to play to your strengths, so do not become defensive in responding. The doctor is wise to ensure that patients are not referred to a charlatan. There may also need to be a discussion about whether any information will be shared between you about patients, and if so, what type of material, or under what circumstances.

You may have other strengths. For example, could you run a group at the surgery for patients with eating disorders, or adult survivors of abuse? Unless you suggest possibilities, they will probably not occur to the GP.

It can be quite difficult to actually get to see the GP, so have a backup plan. The practice manager may well be your way in. If you can arrange an appointment to see them, and convince them that what you have to offer will enhance the practice, then they will often be in a better position to put your case to the GP. They also are likely to be the people who manage referrals to you, so it is worth cultivating this relationship.

Another aspect concerns which GP practices you are going to approach. It may be tempting to start with your own GP, as you may well feel that you are more likely to get a sympathetic hearing. While this could be true, there might be some difficulties here. If your practice serves a small community, you could find that there are boundary issues in the referrals – people you know or are very likely to come across at social occasions. At a more pragmatic level, there is a greater risk of bumping into your clients in the local shops if you take referrals from your immediate area. This may be fine by you, but think it through first.

Even if you have worked hard and professionally to obtain referrals from a number of GPs, you will probably find that it takes time for this to turn into more than the odd one or two clients. Thistle (1998) says that counsellors and psychotherapists often say that they have tried without success to obtain such referrals. It is worth staying in touch though, and not giving up on the relationship. Send any new information about your work regularly so that you remain in the forefront. Once the referrals do begin, you may well find that this is a useful part of your work. Useful advice comes from David.

> **David**: I had tried and tried to get referrals through GP surgeries, but nothing much seemed to happen. Then, as often happens, I suggested to a client that they made an appointment with their GP to check out some physical symptoms. A few weeks later, someone rang me to ask about counselling, and said their GP had given them my name – the same GP. So I wrote to her, thanking
>
> ⏵

> her for the referral, and sending some new leaflets. Magically, so it seemed, I began to get referrals through that source. Oddly, and I don't know if there is any connection – do GPs network with each other? – some of the other practices where I'd had no success also began to refer. It's now quite a good part of my client base.

Employee assistance programmes (EAPs)

Many major companies have contracts with EAPs to provide a range of benefits for their employees, such as financial advice, legal advice and health services, including counselling. The EAP then employs independent counsellors and/or psychologists to provide the counselling sessions. These are usually short-term contracts of three to eight sessions. Often, there is a clause in the contract barring the counsellor from entering into a private arrangement at the end of these sessions. This may specify 'not ever', or state that it may not happen within a specific period, such as three months after the EAP work has ended. Some counsellors find this untenable, and if this is the case, they are better not to work with EAPs.

However, for many independent counsellors, this work is a very useful source of clients. Most EAPs will assess clients, often using an affiliate who is a psychologist, before referring them to counsellors, and are clear about what is the main issue to be dealt with, and what particular approach they are expecting to be used – CBT, integrative etc. If the counsellor uncovers other major issues during the course of their work with the client, they need to consider what referral options are available to the client to focus on those issues. Often feedback forms from the counsellor to the EAP have a section that asks about this aspect.

The majority of EAPs employ counsellors accredited already with one of the professional associations, and once statutory professional registration comes into force, almost certainly, they will only employ people who are registered. For them, this gives some measure of assurance of the professional competence of the counsellors to whom they refer clients. There are other, better, reasons for becoming accredited, but, for the independent practitioner, this may be the one that spurs them into accreditation. Very occasionally, if you are not accredited, work may be offered, but usually only if no other counsellor is available at that time in your area, or a particular specialism is required. It will help if you can at least honestly declare that you are in the process of submitting your accreditation documents.

In some contracts between organizations and EAPs, there may be a particular need for counsellors who will work with specific areas. For example, EAPs may include debriefing or trauma work as part of their contract with police forces or fire services. Alternatively, there may be a focus on addiction issues, where this might affect health and safety, such as in the case of warehouse employees or delivery drivers. If you have such a specialism, you may find that this is a useful addition to your normal work with EAP clients.

The contract you will have is between yourself and the EAP. It is very unlikely that you will have any contact with the company for whom your client works. This leaves you free to deal with the client, without involving yourself in organizational issues. In a few cases, this can also be frustrating. You may realize from the volume of clients presenting from one department of one company that there is a particular systemic or managerial problem, i.e. it is not the client who fundamentally has the problem, but the company itself. Should this happen, it is worth bringing this to the attention of a case manager within the EAP, and they may be able to feed that back to the company.

Case managers are the people with whom you have most contact when working for an EAP. Obviously, there are effective and less effective case managers, but in our experience, most are well trained professionals, who are prepared to discuss client issues with you. Indeed, some EAPs make it a requirement that you do discuss your work with them, possibly after a first session and/or at the end of counselling. The relationship is an important one, and pragmatically, how you develop it may affect how many clients are referred to you. A difficulty in doing this may be that at the times you are available to talk to a case manager, during client gaps, they may well not be available, or already on the phone. When leaving messages for them, be clear about when you are available to save unnecessary 'answer phone tag'. This avoids unnecessary time and frustration on both sides.

Although clients have not had the opportunity to choose their counsellor freely, simply being allocated to someone by the EAP, in most cases this does not create problems. Clients are aware that it is not their company that has done the choosing, so are less concerned about what is said by whom to whom. However, as reporting forms have to be submitted to the EAP at the end of counselling, it is imperative to talk through with the client what these might contain. Generally, they are brief forms, with dates attended, presenting issue, focus of the work and outcomes. Some counsellors choose to share what they have written with the client, making this part of the final session's work. In most cases, the EAP will only use the various forms for their own internal auditing, but if a specific report on the counselling is to be sent back to the company by the EAP, it makes ethical sense to ensure that the client knows this.

CORE forms at the beginning and end of counselling are being used increasingly by EAPS to evaluate client progress. Often they will offer free training on using this system, so it is a good opportunity for CPD, as well as to network within the EAP. There is usually a client evaluation form. This is either handed to the counsellor in a sealed envelope at the end of counselling or sent back by the client directly to the EAP.

Hudson-Allez (2007) puts forward a number of reasons against the independent practitioner engaging in EAP work. These include:

- inappropriate contractual obligations;
- demanding that counsellors give priority to EAP clients;
- the implications of data protection when reports are posted (or e-mailed);
- a small share of the fee the EAP actually charges the company;
- level of administration work required.

While acknowledging the validity of these criticisms, in our experience, the better EAPs do work ethically and professionally with their affiliate counsellors, and for the best interests of clients. Our advice would to approach a number of EAPs and discover what is involved. Then choose to apply only to those whose values and ways of working match your own.

> **Suzie**: I'm debating whether to try and get myself on to EAPs' books now that I'm accredited. What do you guys think?
>
> **David**: I used to work with them, but I've stopped now as I got fed up with the paperwork, and all those phone calls. It just felt not worth it.
>
> **Ellie**: Yes, the paperwork can be a pain, but I find they are a useful source of clients, and there is some backup from case managers if I am unsure about anything. They pay me less than I charge private clients, but then I am not having to do the assessments, or actually find the clients.
>
> **Carole**: I have learned to say no when I haven't the space or when I think I'm not suitable for a particular client. I used to worry that the EAP would never contact me again if I said 'no', but they do.
>
> ▐▶

> **Suzie**: Are there some EAPs that you think are better than others?
>
> **Carole and Ellie** (together): Yes!

For obvious reasons, we are not including the rest of the conversation where particular EAPs were discussed, recommended and pulled apart. However, the discussion centred on the attitude of the case managers and front line staff to affiliate counsellors, the support when there were problems, the ease of getting through by telephone, the type more than the amount of paperwork and the pay scale.

Training agencies

These include colleges, universities and independent training organizations. Before you make contact with them, try to discover as much as you can about the courses they run. For example, does their level of training and their orientation match your own? Are the trainers, tutors and courses well regarded? You do not necessarily want to be linked with a course that does not run good professional courses, simply to enhance your income. It might work against you in some other quarters.

Having established that you would be pleased to work with them, decide what you would like to offer. A blanket approach of 'I can do anything' may not bring in any work! If trainees are expected to undertake personal therapy during the course, ask if they are provided with a list of approved counsellors, and how you might be included in that register. The same would apply to supervision of trainees' work. This could be provided in groups in course time and/or there may be a list of supervisors approved to provide external supervision for those whose placement supervision hours would not ensure that trainees meet the minimum number of supervised hours required by the training establishment.

If you have previous experience as a trainer, you might consider working part-time on a local certificate or diploma course. An alternative could be offering to present one-off workshops during a training course on a particular area of expertise – sexual abuse, working with suicidal clients or addiction, for example.

If you undertake to be part of a course team on a part-time basis, do build in extra time for this. Obviously, there is travel time, but in addition, there may well be course meetings, tutorials, marking and moderation. These extra hours can mount up, so try to discover what might be involved and how you would be paid for these activities before committing yourself. The fees are not particularly high, but can be a useful and regular addition to other income.

> **Ellie**: I love working on the certificate course. To be with people who are taking their first steps into using counselling skills can be magic. Just watching them blossom is so rewarding. It gives me a buzz I don't get in the rest of my work. I also get the support of my colleagues in the team, and I have to say that I have also had a number of clients and supervisees through this work – not people actually on the course, obviously, but their friends.

Other agencies

There are other agencies and organizations that might be prepared to refer clients to you. These include occupational health and human resource departments of large companies, local authorities, social services, voluntary organizations and charities who have clients with a specific issue – often health related. Some faith-based organizations also seek secular counsellors, though obviously here it is imperative that if you do not hold the same faith you are not antipathetic towards it.

If you can provide supervision or training, then it is worth approaching counselling agencies to offer your services. Even the voluntary organizations are prepared to pay external providers for these services. You may have to have a fee scale that includes a low-cost or voluntary organization rate, but it can still be a reasonable source of income, and also helps to get your name known in the area. Doing this type of work can often bring in client referrals at a later date. You may feel able to train groups of employees within companies in 'people skills', as well as working as a coach or mentor for individual employees. Try thinking outside the box to see what areas you might be interested in developing.

It can take large amounts of time and energy to develop these contacts. If you do this halfheartedly, you are unlikely to succeed, so do think carefully before rushing into a large number of possible leads. It could be worth you deciding that you want to concentrate on one area at a time – supervision, working with siblings of children with life-limiting illnesses or training, for example. Then put the time and energy you have available into making contacts and marketing yourself. We have said more about marketing in Chapter 8. It is sufficient here to remind you that your time, at the early stages of being in independent practice, is valuable. You may have more of it at this point, but you want to use it wisely and productively. It is also worth bearing in mind that contacts can take a very long time to develop into actual work, so do not feel disheartened if initially all your best efforts are not resulting in very much income.

Suzie: It is sometimes hard to know where to find possible leads for work. Any ideas?

Belinda: You could use Yellow Pages to discover the large organizations in the area and approach them. I began by listing all the counselling agencies I knew of and then asked friends and colleagues to add to them.

David: You've got a social services background, so why not make them aware that you are able to take clients referred by them. You'll need to establish that this is a fee paying service, and find out who would be responsible for payments, though, otherwise it could be a muddle.

Carole: I listen carefully to conversations around me to discover names and positions of people who might be good contacts. That sounds dreadful put like that, but I have picked up some useful contacts!

David: Do we know if the hospital provides a specialism? Sometimes hospitals do refer people for counselling. Could be worth a try.

Ellie: I keep meaning to approach local and national charities to see if they run support services or counselling. It does take time to do all these things.

Suzie: That's really helpful. I'm constantly surprised how generous people are with their contacts and information. Thanks.

Information sources and backup

As you set up your practice, it is valuable to begin to compile a list of specialist agencies to which you might turn for information or advice, or indeed refer clients on. This can be added to as you find new ones – and obviously kept up to date. Contacting these agencies and possibly visiting them will help you know which one might be the right one to contact if you need to do so. They will often have leaflets that you might want to pass on to your clients. Agencies might include those dealing with psychosexual issues, addiction, abuse or children. Even if clients do not need this information for themselves, as McMahon et al. (2005) point out, it may be appreciated as a source of help and advice for someone close to them.

Medical backup

Establishing good links within the medical profession is wise for two reasons. The more obvious one is in the hope of referrals, as we have explored above. The second is that it will give you access to information and advice about treatments, medication and specific client issues that you may know less about. In addition, some professional organizations require you to state in your application for membership or accreditation that you do have access to medical consultancy.

Through your local NHS, you could make contact with consultant psychiatrists. Some independent practitioners decide that they will undertake a voluntary placement within a psychiatric department. This enhances their knowledge and experience in a wide range of mental health issues, and in addition gives closer contact with known psychiatrists if you need to seek expert support concerning one of your own clients.

You could decide that in addition to counselling supervision, it would be valuable to have regular, though probably less frequent, supervision with a psychiatrist or counselling psychologist. This gives you an opportunity for more in-depth consideration of mental health issues. At the very least, it helps to have established a contact, so you can consult 'as and when' you need to do so.

Contact with GPs is another useful medical backup. You may decide that you will routinely ask clients for their GP name and practice details when you do your intake forms. Not all practitioners want to do this, and if you decide it is useful information, you need to discuss with the client your reasons for asking this, and under what circumstances you would contact the GP. It can be helpful for GPs to know that their patients are undertaking counselling or psychotherapy, though some clients may not want this on their medical records, so it is a sensitive area. However, since physical and emotional health are so closely linked, it is worth consideration, particularly if there is suicidal ideation.

To be able to talk with a GP can help you feel less isolated in your work and ensure that the client has the best care possible. It can also be useful to discover more about a particular medical condition or medication side effects, though you may prefer searching on the Internet to discover these. In most cases, it is ethical only to consult with a GP if you have the client's permission to do so. In many more situations, it can be more helpful to ask the client to visit their GP if you feel it is necessary, and possibly for them to inform the doctor that they are seeing you. An example would be when you feel that the use of antidepressants might enable a client to engage more in the sessions. Another case might be when you are not sure if something is due to emotional or physical conditions – is the overwhelming lethargy related to a stressful personal situation, or to an underlying medical condition?

CONTINUING PROFESSIONAL DEVELOPMENT (CPD)

Most professional bodies, such as the HPC, UKCP and BACP, require that practitioners must be able to evidence personal and professional CPD to retain membership or accreditation As well as being necessary to update knowledge and skills, these activities can have the added bonus of bringing enjoyment and refreshment to the independent practitioner (Symes, 1994). It is an opportunity to meet and network with other professionals, and reduce feelings of isolation. Talking over coffee or lunch is as much CPD in some cases as the actual content of the course or workshop.

One of the downsides of CPD is that you now have to finance that yourself. Independent practitioners often have to make hard choices about where they spend their money. There are different reasons for deciding on an activity. These include:

- needing to find out more about a specific area of your work because of a particular client or client group you are working with;
- being interested in or attracted to a new development in your field;
- wanting to deepen your knowledge of an area, e.g. psychosis;
- developing new skills;
- wanting to do a 'taster' session before you decide about longer-term training, e.g. with couples;
- it fits in with a CPD plan you have worked out with your mentor.

There may also be pragmatic reasons such as:

- the CPD is low-cost or free;
- it is in your area;
- it sounds lively and interesting;
- you have heard good reports about the trainers.

Not all CPD activities have to be costly. You might set up or join a group of like-minded professionals, and use meetings to discuss new research findings, a particular issue, a newly published book or aspects of independent practice. Some such groups will ask a local 'expert' to join them for a meeting, and while there is usually a fee involved in this, it is likely to be quite small when divided by the number of group members.

Local associations of professionals also provide CPD in the form of their meetings. For an annual cost, and perhaps a small fee per attendance, they may offer evenings where there is a speaker and, as well, another opportunity to network. Even if you do not think the particular topic for that month is of vital interest to you, it is often worth going for the contact with others – and who knows, you may surprise yourself by learning something new or interesting about the topic of the meeting!

There are some other ways of undertaking CPD, including reading professional journals and books, or carrying out research into an area that interests you. Research can mean either simply discovering more about something entirely for your own use, or undertaking more formal and in-depth research, possibly including other participants, and publishing it, or sharing your findings with colleagues. If you are going to include reading or private research as part of your CPD activities, it is not enough simply to state as evidence 'Reading journals – fifty hours'. While this may be accurate, you may need to supply evidence of those fifty hours if, for example, your reaccreditation documents are subject to a random audit. What did you read, and how did you use, or reflect on, the reading? We find we need to keep a record of what we have done, so that we remember and can demonstrate this to others.

For many practitioners, in some periods of their independent practice, personal therapy may be undertaken, and this can be included as part of your CPD in most psychological professions. It is costly, so some practitioners will choose not to undertake this, reasoning that during their training or earlier professional life, they have 'done enough therapy to sort out any of their own issues'. However, most of us will come across clients who trigger or re-trigger our own issues, and there could be life events that cause us to want to undertake more. In these circumstances, it is of benefit to re-engage in personal work. Indeed, because starting and maintaining an independent practice is stressful, that in itself may be a time when we seek this support.

PEER SUPPORT

Several references have already been made to peer support as a valuable component of maintaining a successful practice. So how do you go about getting this? As has been mentioned above, joining a local association or network is one way. If you know of other independent practitioners in your area, make contact with them, and discover if they meet together – if not, perhaps you could be an initiator of a support group.

If you have qualified fairly recently, or have just undertaken further training, there may be an opportunity to develop a support system from among other trainees. Anne is still a member of a group set up twenty-five years ago when we finished initial training. We continue to meet several times a year all over the UK. Some members have dropped out over the years, and all of us have changed to and from employment and self-employment at times. However, we still gain practical and emotional professional support, as well as challenge, from each other. The mixture of employed and independent practitioners has also worked well. We learn from each other, and keep up to date with settings other than our own, so do not discount peer support from a range of sources.

Peer support groups can be a source of referrals. It is often helpful to give enquirers contact details for people you know and whose work you trust, if you cannot take a new client at that time. People in your networks will do the same for you.

They can also be a source of information. Colleagues may know more than you about an agency, an issue that a client is bringing, current research or where you can obtain further advice and support. The time taken out of client work for meeting with peers is usually time well spent. If you find it is not, widen or change your support network.

SUPERVISION

As Symes (1994) states, in independent practice taking care of oneself is vital, and supervision is one of the ways of doing so. You no longer have colleagues on tap to 'have a brief word with', or to gently tell you when you are becoming stressed or overworked. So having a good supervisor, who can look at all aspects of your work, including the practical parts of running a business, is crucial. Often practitioners think that the more experienced they become, the less supervision they need. However, when you start your practice, you become a novice again in some respects, and may find yourself in various places on the grid in Figure 11.1. This may vary

Unconscious incompetence	Conscious incompetence
Conscious competence	Unconscious competence

Figure 11.1 The grid of competence.

almost from day to day as you face different challenges. So you may find yourself back in the conscious incompetent or conscious competent areas of the grid at times. Remind yourself that this is part of the normal development of the independent practitioner as you take on new challenges.

For this reason, think about your choice of supervisor carefully. You need to be able to trust that person enough to be open about what is happening, not only in your client work, but also about how you are managing such things as workload, support and income. Some of the considerations influencing your choice might be:

■ Has she experience of working independently?
■ Do you trust her advice and judgement?
■ Do you feel safe enough to uncover your 'warts'?
■ Can you offload and moan when you need to do so?
■ Is her theoretical approach more important than her business experience, or vice versa?
■ Has she been established long enough to have knowledge of local services you might want to plug into?
■ How available is she out of normal supervision contact time?
■ Does she keep herself up to date with current developments in your field?
■ Can she challenge you in a way that you can hear?
■ Will she encourage you to develop your own internal supervisor?

Rather more pragmatically a colleague just entering independent practice added the following.

> **Suzie:** I can afford her rates if I need extra supervision. She lives near enough to make my travelling to supervision simple.
>
> ⮕

> Another independent practitioner recommended her. And I like
> her, and if I am going to spend time with her regularly over the
> next few years, that feels important!

Since your supervisor is 'an indispensible part of the helper's ongoing self-development, self-awareness and commitment to development' (Hawkins & Shohet 2000), making the relationship is a serious business, and it is worth having an initial meeting with a number of possible supervisors before making your choice. We may often say this to clients when they first make a contact with us about choosing a counsellor, but forget our own advice when choosing our supervisor.

One other option would be to seek peer supervision, either one-to-one or in a group. This is obviously more cost effective. It could have an additional bonus if you could join, or establish a group, made up of professionals in different but related fields. These might include counsellors, psychotherapists, psychologists and psychiatrists. Each discipline can learn from each other, and contribute different understandings of an issue, as well as being a handy source of both clients and expert information.

However, there are also downsides to a peer group. It can become collusive or competitive, or simply become stale and a chat group. Without clear structures and a supervisor, it can fall apart. Members may feel less committed to a group of peers than to a supervisor they pay, so attendance rates may vary. Of course, conversely, sometimes people feel more committed to a group of peers.

As we have stated earlier, there are other people who can support you, even though they may not initially come into your mind when you consider peer support. These include business mentors, lawyers and accountants. Cultivate your relationships with them.

MANAGING YOUR DIARY

The last practical aspect of running your practice that we explore here is how to manage your diary. One of the heartfelt cries often heard among independent practitioners is that their diary has run away with them – in other words, the diary is managing them. This definitely includes us at times!

When you made your business plan, you would have estimated how many clients, supervisees, assessment sessions, training etc. you would need each week or each month in order to break even, pay the mortgage and put food on the table. Then on top of that, you would have considered what would be reasonable in terms of 'extras' to maintain the standard of living you want to enjoy. A fine plan, and life is not always like that.

In the first months of independent practice, it is understandable that if work comes your way, you do not wish to turn it away. There is a fear that this might be the last referral you receive, or that you may not be asked ever again to input on a course if you turn down this opportunity. This may be fine in the early days. You have enough space in your diary to take on things, and you are prepared at this stage to have early mornings and late evening appointments because there are gaps in the rest of the day to attend to the business aspects, write client notes and do such mundane things as eat.

Taking on everything can become a habit, and not a very healthy one. We can find surprisingly quickly that we do not have any gaps; our days are too long and there is no time to relax or socialize. This can lead to disenchantment, which in turn may lead to poor practice.

So try to take time to think about accepting new work. Learn to say 'no' to the client enquirer who says that the only time they could see you is at 8 p.m. on a Friday evening, if that is way beyond the time you intended to work. It may mean that they choose to find someone else, but they may also suddenly discover that there are other manageable times. Indeed, therapeutically, you could be colluding with their underlying issue of not managing their own lifestyle if you take them on at the time they request.

If something does not need an immediate answer, remember all the assertiveness techniques you encourage clients to use. 'I will need to take time to think about this' or 'Thank you for asking me to do this. I will get back to you tomorrow to let you know if I am able to do so' are useful stock phrases. Then you can look calmly at your other commitments and make an informed decision about how you want to manage your workload and your diary.

CONCLUSION

In concluding this chapter, we encourage you to remember that life is not all about work. There does need to be a balance. In the long run, your friends and family are more important to you than individual contracts. That is not to say that once you have committed yourself to a contract you should not fulfil it professionally and to the best of your ability. It is just a word of warning that even those people around you, who have most actively encouraged you to take the step into independent practice, can get a little exasperated eighteen months down the line, when you are too busy to spend any time with them. Believe it – we know!

Reflexive Points

You may want to undertake one or more of the following activities to review how you run your practice.

- If you would consider working with EAP clients, visit a number of websites or contact them directly, to discover whether their requirements fit with you, before contacting them.
- Review your existing contacts with the medical profession. Notice the gaps and think how you might go about filling these.
- Begin to compile a list of referral agencies and organizations that you could offer to clients.
- Make a list, or a mind map, of other skills you have, such as training, coaching and mentoring. Then add in possible places or means of obtaining work with them.
- Review your current supervision arrangements. In what ways do they support your independent practice, and are there any things you want or need that are missing?
- What are the areas in which you want to undertake CPD activities during the next year? How will these enhance your practice and/or professional development?

Chapter 12

Reflections on Private Practice

INTRODUCTION

The concluding chapter of a practical book such as this can be a dilemma. The main points have been covered in previous chapters, and there is a risk of simply repeating much of what has been said. Like many writers, we had left decisions about what we wanted to say in the final chapter until we had completed the drafts of the other chapters. As we talked together, we realized that what was missing was the narrative of how independent practice actually might look like in reality. As a result, we recorded a conversation about our own experiences, and have transcribed it below.

We do not offer this as 'the right approach' or think that our thoughts will necessarily be shared by all our readers. We have kept in our asides and the comments that may raise eyebrows, because we wanted to be authentic and congruent. Since we will not be present with you as you read it, to answer questions or explain more fully, we simply hope that it will take your thinking about independent practice further. You may agree with comments or disagree violently with them, but if it takes your sense of how *you* want to shape your own practice then it will have succeeded.

You will see that neither of us came into independent practice with a well thought out business plan, or marketing strategies, as we have recommended in previous chapters. That does not mean that we do not believe what we have written. We were living in a different time, and there were no texts around to help us think out how we wanted to begin and develop.

OUR REFLECTIONS

Robert: Anne, it may be interesting for readers to know how you came into the field of working independently as a therapist.

Anne: All was happenstance initially. I worked for twenty years in secondary education before I trained as a counsellor. Then I was training counsellors in an institution and getting some private referrals. I (a) got very tired of working in an organization and the politics etc., which felt nothing to do with the work that I was doing, and (b) I was getting enough referrals that I wanted to be able to space them out a bit more and not feel under pressure. So I did what a lot of practitioners do I think, and became part-time employed and part-time self-employed. Then that got a bit out of hand because I was asked to do more and more training independently and I realized that I couldn't cope with still being employed.

So, I suppose after a period of about two years, I half-reluctantly said goodbye to pension and half a steady income and took the step of becoming self-employed and really have never regretted it. Nearing perhaps the end of my professional life, I might regret the lack of pension, but I don't, that's a minor thing. And it has evolved. People have asked me to do things and I thought 'mm, might like to do that'. The whole practice evolved in terms of actually where I practised; I initially practised in a rented building and that was both expensive and took time out going to it and trying to block clients together etc. So I then started working from a room at home, and eventually built an extension which is my counselling room and has a loo en suite etc., etc.

All those things just make life so much easier. We refer somewhere to clients having to walk through your house and doors open or keeping rooms tidy and things – it is lovely having a separate bit, I really like that. And it was great fun planning it as well. What about you?

Robert: I think much the same as you. I started life as a practising clinical psychologist around twenty-five years ago now, and again, similar to yourself, I started getting involved in seeing the very occasional client who wanted to be seen at different times or specifically wanted to be seen by me and that was really the evolution of it.

I never sat down and planned a private practice in the way that we've tried to describe in the book and, as we're only too aware, there is only so little to guide you in all of this and so therefore

⁗➡

your own experience, talking to other people, case law, anything that you can grab in terms of an idea, has always been helpful.

I have to say quite a lot of that has actually been from outside of my counselling/psychotherapy/psychology training. It's been from related areas. I've seen how successful people run businesses. I have friends who do similar work, but obviously not necessary client-based, but it may be that they are selling a particular product, and there are really quite important and significant overlaps which I found helpful.

I'm really pleased that you mentioned something, which I'm sure so many readers would be delighted hear, and that is that the size of your practice 'got out of hand'. I think that's how we all want things to be – that things get bigger to the point that we have to make choices and, hopefully, those are positive choices to make, and that is how to thin down on the activity that we're involved in so as to concentrate on the things either that we enjoy or potentially are the ones that help us to earn a living. That's a more pragmatic response. I've tried to keep a number of different areas of interest active. I think that's a reflection of me and my personality. I think that working one setting or context, or with one group of clients, I might find interesting but perhaps insufficient to keep me stimulated over a long period of time. So I do some work in schools, I see people independently or privately after work, and I also do some work in one or two niche areas, particularly in the airline industry.

Unlike you – and I have to say I'm envious – I see clients from home and so all of the difficulties that we've described in the book I'm only too keenly aware of, particularly the almost dual side of you that you present to the client. Somebody coming into your home obviously must associate it with professional activity, but they will attribute certain things to you personally, which I'm aware of. Maybe I'm fortunate in that most of the clients I see have been referred, they've been through some kind of 'screening process' by the referrers, which is helpful, so I don't feel as anxious about people who come to me, but certainly it's an evolving practice.

Anne: I think one of the key things there is how you're trained and what your view – or my view – is of clients knowing things about myself. With our extension, they obviously see the garden and might make some judgements about me and gardens or whatever. If you can furnish your own rented rooms, this probably still applies, but it certainly applies at home – the choice of furniture, they know it's you, it's not some bureaucratic organi-

IIII➡

zation. And I guess for some people that's really difficult. I wouldn't want to have family photographs in my counselling room etc., etc., but I'm aware that the choice of the curtain material, the choice of colour, may say something.

Robert: I have become much more aware of how those attributions may affect the whole process of therapy – I think I've got to a point now where I feel comfortable about those issues, though I am aware of them. So when choosing furniture, or indeed a car, since patients or clients may see a car, or a new car, outside, I would think very carefully about that. I'm certainly aware of it. But I feel much less reticent about doing things, worrying that somehow I'm going to give the wrong message to people.

I'm wondering Anne – I mean, so many people these days work so hard and perhaps feel like they're standing still, especially in the current economic climate. Yet there is always a danger in this kind of area, whether it's one's ambition, whether it's financial need, whether it's just desire to succeed, all of which may be health motivators – how to you know if you're doing too much? How do you know if you're feeling stressed or overstretched in the work you're doing?

Anne: There are two answers to that. The honest answer is that it's when I catch myself tidying things – when I tidy my desk or I clear out the kitchen cupboard – I think that's a sign for me that I need to get some order and space back in my life. So that's actually what happens. Then I look at my diary – and it's not necessarily even just the amount that's in the diary. It may be to do with the diversity of things that I'm doing, because I'm a person who loves new opportunities and tends to take them on without dropping something off the other end (which is bad practice for an independent practitioner and I advise other people not to do that).

If we look at this moment – we're writing this together; I'm rewriting a course for somewhere else; I'm developing some different training as well and also maintaining the other things that I do, the supervision, the online work, the client work etc., etc.

So it's not just how full my diary is, because there may appear to be in one day some sensible little gaps, but actually it's remembering that I've got to do something for the book or something more for the course. I guess I'm talking about blocking out time as well for those things you think are going to take 'just a couple of minutes' and don't! But I know it when I can feel that I'm scrabbling in a heap around me.

Robert: I know those feelings too well! Certainly something that I've experienced is that when I'm not working in the NHS I need to take greater care about how I manage my own time and therefore aspects of my life. When I do more regular salaried employment, I know when the day begins and technically when it ends, although few of us work nine to five these days, we do considerably more.

When I'm working independently, I have some rituals that I need to enjoy, such as going to the gym, going for a walk. When those start to fall by the wayside, that's when my stress levels will increase. So these are really just designed to destress me, change the focus of what I'm doing, try to leave the healthy life that we often encourage our clients to do. But it's when I forgo that or have to book in a client at a particular time that I start to experience stress.

Which made me think a bit too about something that we've stressed quite a lot in the book – how we allocate time to clients. Maybe we didn't emphasize strongly enough how much this must reflect the psychotherapeutic approach of the practitioner. I've been trained and brought up in a style of practice which I think is briefer, more biased towards cognitive and behavioural, focused on particular outcomes that are measurable – not that I'm suggesting this is the right way, but certainly it is a way in which I've been trained – I find that if clients change appointments, that my stress levels may increase if I feel that I have to rebook them at a later point when I have other clients booked in.

I don't have a personal secretary who does this, so I will often find myself contacting clients to see whether they are able to move a session. I'm sure that some readers would be alarmed to hear this and think that this interferes with the therapeutic relationship; that there are set times and sessions where we agree to see clients and that they agree to fit with this. My experience is pragmatic. All of my clients of course live in the real world – they may get caught up in traffic, they may have a member of the family who is unwell, there may be some difficulty in keeping the appointment – and I like to respect their decisions around that and I value their custom and the fact that they want to come to me. But I also have to make it work for me at a practical level. So I've found that I've perhaps 'breached' the convention in therapy, but it seems to work because when I do contact people, they usually are very happy to do some chopping and changing and it hasn't necessarily negatively impacted upon the therapy. I always address this in my supervision sessions. I don't know if you find the same in the different contexts in which you see clients?　　　　⮕

Anne: Absolutely. I sometimes wonder – and this, I know, is heresy – how the same time every week for fifty minutes came about, and I suspect it was probably because that suited people's diaries. And then we had to look for a therapeutic reason. I'm not dismissing that and I think that works very well for some clients and some practitioners. It doesn't work for me all of the time. I have a few clients that I do see regularly and one who I think changing the appointment would cause problems with currently, and as far as humanly possible I try and avoid that.

But the bulk of my clients, it doesn't seem to worry them at all. And I think that's partly because, you don't go to the GP, for example – if you've got to go back for a repeat session – you don't go back at the same time, same day. They've got diaries. A lot of the people I work with are in full-time work and they need to work round meetings etc., and sometimes they are very pleased if it has to be changed, it suits them very well as well.

It's not just them asking me – and again this is heresy – I have to confess to the occasional moment of delight when a client cancels an appointment and I think 'wow, I've got an extra bit of space there'. I'm sure some practitioners, some people reading this book, will be horrified at that, but that's actually the reality of my life, I fit client and supervision sessions round training, external examining etc. Online work is great because that is slightly more flexible and I can, on the whole, fit that round existing commitments.

Robert: I'm relieved to hear about your flexibility in approach because I think many people who practise as therapists are taught to do so in a way that is fairly predictable and formulaic and I think as soon as we break beyond the certain expectations or models or practice 'rules', we start to feel anxious. But in independent practice, it requires us to bring together so many different ideas, it's not just about the therapeutic approach you're using, it's also about the management of your time, the management of your livelihood, the management of your family time and so on. And I think if we approach it in an inflexible way, we're not going to enjoy it as much and we probably will have more stress.

Anne: I was just thinking as well, I want to be flexible – the thing I don't want to do is to be *too* flexible. I see clients from quarter to eight in the morning and now I tend to finish by seven, but there have been times when it's been later, and I don't want to have a day when I work solidly through that time. Apart from that, I can't do it any longer – that's an ageing thing, I think. And I certainly wouldn't want five days a week of that. So as well as being flexible, I've also got to build in things around me like the gym that you were talking about etc.

⟶

Robert: And also you've mentioned something maybe about ourselves individually and where we are in our own life cycle or development. Of course, our interests grow and develop and that pertains both to our professional interests as well as what's going on in our personal lives. It may be that people reading this book will be at different stages. I suppose I would define myself as being mid-career in terms of both my age and how long I've practised for, but I foresee a time where I would perhaps want to work less than I do at the moment. I'd want to focus on certain things more than on others, where perhaps I would want to move to another level and do more supervisory training work or teaching, as opposed to only seeing clients in different contexts or settings.

I think that is important because each of us, at different points of this life cycle, will have different interests and some of those, of course, are constrained by what's going on in the wider economy – things that we might have had ambitions about have perhaps had to be put on hold. But nonetheless, I think that it must reflect something about what we're capable of doing in our own personal lives. And that, I think, makes it quite an exciting place to work; we don't have to work at the same rate, the same pace, with the same clients and not necessarily using the same models. Whereas in salaried or employed conditions, there may be more constraints because other people may be dictating those.

Anne: The readers can't see us, but if they could, they'd know that I'm obviously at a different place in the life cycle, my career cycle! I don't feel anywhere near the end of it, but I must accept that I am moving probably *towards* the end of it, and I've chosen now to work three days a week – and that's great. The difficulty with that, of course, is avoiding cramming the days, but it's wonderful to have the flexibility to do that. I might not be able to do that in paid employment.

I can do as much or as little as I want, I can still take on new things, I can drop some things off the end as well. I think some of the things that you have to consider very seriously are things like long-term work and long-term training and, for that reason, I suspect I will probably not take on any clients now that I can see might be with me for years, because I think that would probably be unethical on my part. I probably wouldn't start developing a new course that would take perhaps two years to develop and get through various bodies, that I'd want to be around for the first three or four years before handing it on to somebody else.

III➤

So there are constraints in terms of your life cycle – which you might not get if you were employed because you might have to do it regardless of whether you were going to be out of the business, into retirement in two years, because that's part of your job description. So there are different ethical issues, I guess.

Robert: I think that's very helpful. Maybe having an end point in mind, even if it's at the start of your career, is quite important because it helps you to shape where you're going to, to get an idea of what the journey's going to look like, even if it needs to change route or course, and ultimately what you're aiming for. Clearly we need to respond flexibly to all of these ideas, but exactly as you said, the metaphor for therapy applies. Any final words or thoughts?

Anne: I was thinking as we were both talking about how we got into doing this – I've been twenty-five years, you twenty something I think you said – I think things are different now. We did have to make it up as we went along, and that's still to some extent true, but I think it now has to be much better thought out and worked with than when we started. I guess the other thing is that it's been really useful writing this book, because it's actually made me recognize what I do do – and maybe what I don't do – and there may be something about that.

Robert: I'm pleased you've highlighted that because I've learnt a lot from writing the book, especially the idea of going to different sources to try and help all of us to understand what are the essential things that we need for setting up and developing a practice. Whether these relate to practical matters or perhaps those relating to how we practise and how we choose to relate to clients, all of which I think is important. I certainly find that in my independent practice, I enjoy therapeutic work much more, I find the challenges more frequent, I feel more personally responsible for managing those challenges, I suppose, than I do to a committee of people in another context in which I work.

And I've also noticed as I look back – and I think this has been helped by our conversations – where I work, how I work and the methods that I use keep evolving and I think, to be a therapist who is changing, I find exciting, it renews my interest in what I do and I find that much more in my independent practice than in any other context. And so I like to think that for somebody who shares my time between independent practice and salaried practice the one actually helps the other in many different ways.

CONCLUSION

As you will have gathered from our conversation, both of us are passionate about our independent practices. If you are not, it is likely to be more of an uphill struggle, and bring you less satisfaction, even if you do make a good financial living. We hope that we have encouraged you to use your passion to shape and develop your individual independent practice, which will be different from everyone else's. However, sadly, passion by itself is unlikely to be sufficient in the current climate of an ever-increasing independent sector. So do take the time to plan, to evaluate and to develop so that your business will go from strength to strength. We wish you success.

References

Anderson, W. (1998) Boardroom. *Networker* January/February: 35–41.

Bond, T. & Mitchels, B. (2008) *Confidentiality and Record Keeping in Counselling and Psychotherapy*. London: Sage.

Bor, R., Gill, S., Miller, R. & Parrot, C. (2004) *Doing Therapy Briefly*. Basingstoke: Palgrave Macmillan.

Corrie, S. & Lane, D. (2006) Constructing stories about clients' needs: developing skills in formulation. In R. Bor & M. Watts (eds), *The Trainee Handbook*. London: Sage.

Cristofoli, G. (2002) Legal pitfalls in counselling and psychotherapy practice and how to avoid them. In P. Jenkins (ed.), *Legal Issues in Counselling and Psychotherapy*. London: Sage.

Field, R. (2007) Working from home in independent practice. In A. Hemmings & R. Field (eds), *Counselling and Psychotherapy in Contemporary Private Practice*. Hove: Routledge.

Hawkins, P. & Shohet, R. (2000) *Supervision in the Helping Professions*, 2nd edn. Maidenhead: Open University Press.

Haley, J. (1976) *Problem-Solving Therapy*. San Francisco: Jossey-Bass.

Hemmings, A. & Field, R. (eds) (2007) *Counselling and Psychotherapy in Contemporary Private Practice*. Hove: Routledge.

Hudson-Allez, G. (2007) The changing status of counselling. In A. Hemmings & R. Field (eds), *Counselling and Psychotherapy in Contemporary Private Practice*. Hove: Routledge.

Jenkins, P. (ed.) (2002) *Legal Issues in Counselling and Psychotherapy*. London: Sage.

Jones, C. (2009a) Marketing Toolbox – a call to action. *Therapy Today* February: 15.

Jones, C. (2009b) Marketing Toolbox – a brand new you? *Therapy Today* April: 13.

Jones, G. & Stokes, A. (2009) *Online Counselling: A Handbook for Practitioners*. Basingstoke: Palgrave Macmillan.

McMahon, G., Palmer, S. & Wilding, C. (2005) *The Essential Skills for Setting up a Counselling and Psychotherapy Practice*. London: Routledge.

Miller, R. (2006) The first session with a new client. In R. Bor & M. Watts (eds), *The Trainee Handbook*. London: Sage.

Symes, G. (1994) *Counselling in Independent Practice*. Buckingham: Open University Press.

Thistle, R. (1998) *Counselling and Psychotherapy in Private Practice*. London: Sage.

Travilla, C. (1990) *Caring without Wearing: A Small Group Discussion Guide*. Denver, CO: NavPress.

Towergate News (2009) Risks of working from home. *Towergate Professional Risks* August.

Tyler, R. (2003) *Money Matters for Therapists: A Financial Guide for Self-employed Therapists and Counsellors*. London: Worth Press.

Index